FROM STRESS TO SUCCESS

THE ABC OF STRESS MANAGEMENT

Copyright © Jason Sandler

Jason Sandler has his right to be identified as the author of this work in accordance with all legal Copyright Acts

ISBN 978-0-620-86580-7

Acknowledgments

I owe a huge debt of gratitude to all those that made this book possible.

Carol-Ann Savosnick for the editing, Glen Isserow and Tertius for helping with the amazing cover, Adele du Rand for being my grammarian of note, each and every person who believed enough in me to help financially.

Back A Buddy for seeing my vision and allowing me onto your crowd-funding platform.

I would also like to thank those of you that kept me on track and kept me accountable and, for all the support I received from both my Master Mind group and my mentors, Arnie and Don. Let's not forget Neil for being my constant ear-worm.

I thank you all.

A special mention must go to my ex-wives (yes that's plural) for teaching me both what stress is and how to manage it!

Table of Contents

Introduction

"Stress is an ignorant state. It believes that everything is an emergency. Nothing is that important. Just lie down." - Natalie Goldberg

As we all have to know, the world goes through some exciting transitions every few years. For example, think of the advent of electricity and what changes that created in the world. And every new transition brings with it corresponding feelings of either great enthusiasm, or great trepidation, or maybe even a bit of both, depending on which side of the fence you're sitting.

I'm confident that my philosophies will always choose to look at things from a positive perspective and I have this strong belief that I'm not alone in this.. Sadly, though, many more people tend to take the negative view and look at things from a purely negative perspective..

The world is full of pessimistic people. People who will often state that it is far better to be negative and then be surprised when something good happens, than be positive and then become all negative and despondent when it doesn't work out. The problem with these outlooks on life, in my opinion, is that what happens is we are so inundated with negativity that we focus on it more and thereby, start to create even more of it in our lives, as borne out by the saying "Where energy flows, attention goes."

The world today is becoming a smaller and smaller place, and we are spending more and more of our time being busy. Let's forget the fact that we have more machinery that's supposed to make our lives easier; all most of it is doing is opening us up for more "other stuff."

Life most definitely is not nearly as natural as it used to be, not as laid back as it used to be, not as peaceful as it used to be, not, not and let's throw in another not!

Man has always suffered from stress, although the triggers have changed many times throughout history. When we lived in caves, our stress was related to whether we were going to eat or beeaten that day. As life evolved, it was stress that drove us to improve ourselves and the things around us. Solid buildings to protect us when we slept at night, tools to make our tasks more manageable, guns to protect us, and so on.

What has changed then, you may ask?

The way the world is evolving, we are finding it more and more difficult to avoid stressors in our lives. Gone are the days where at five o'clock we put down our tools and went home to enjoy spending time with our families. The advent of mobile phones has led to an attitude of "always available". This is taken to an even higher degree when you realise that this also now overrides time differences all around the world.

So, what can we do about it?

We need to learn to manage it!

If anyone tells you that you need to learn to eliminate stress from your life, look them in the eye and let off a mighty laugh! Impossible. There's no escape.

We live in a world where not being accessible or connected is an extreme rarity. So instead of trying to fight it, let's find a way to embrace stress and make it a positive vibe in our lives rather than a negative influence that's challenging to take back control over.

"The A-Z of Stress Management" is a practical book to help you learn to manage your stress.

Yes, it is your stress. Why may you ask? Because things happen, that's the way life works; whether you choose to allow it to manifest as stress in your life or not is entirely up to you.

In this book, I have taken the alphabet and given each letter an activity that will help you take back control.

This book has specifically been written so that you can randomly open on a page and read the "chapter" in a few moments and then BAM! implement the recommended strategies, and create change in your life

At the end of every chapter, I have purposely left enough space for you to make notes. After all, this is not just a book you're going to read once and toss aside. Nor is it only a training manual; this book is a means to an end. The end of stress being your master!

Chapter 1

What is this thing called stress?

"I promise you nothing is as chaotic as it seems. Nothing is worth diminishing your health. Nothing is worth poisoning yourself into stress, anxiety, and fear."

— Steve Maraboli

Now let us get one thing straight. This book is all about stress management. It can never be about stress elimination, because it is humanly impossible to completely eliminate stress from our lives, no matter how hard we may try. What we can do, rather is to try and find out how we are currently dealing and coping with the stress that we do have to face on a regular and daily basis.

So, where does it all start? Well, it's got to start at the beginning, of course, and that begins with an understanding of exactly what stress is.

You see, people often bandy the word, "stress" about without knowing what stress really is. Yes, we all have our own definition of what stress is, but the definition, from what I consider to be the world's best dictionary – the most authoritative dictionary in the world = which, just by the way, for those that do not know, is called, Jason's Dictionary, is that stress as "a situation where you feel as if you do not have full control."

So, now that we have a definition of stress, it's no wonder that we constantly feel like we're bogged down and completely overloaded with the burden of both physical and mental, to the point where we just feel that we cannot cope and that there is no way to break free.

These demands can be things related to life's everyday routines, such as finances, work, relationships, and other such situations, but really, anything that poses a real or perceived challenge or threat to our well-being can cause us a certain amount of stress.

What I want you to know, however, is that you can learn to manage your stress and not just be constantly looking for ways to eliminate stress from you life entirely. I am here to tell you that you can, in fact, allow your stress to be a motivator for change. After all, in the ancient world, stress was, in fact, essential to our ancestors' survival. The "fight-or-flight" mechanism told early humans when and how to respond to danger. Their adrenalin levels would rise, allowing them to find the strength in their muscles to fight, or the strength in their legs to run away. However, modern man is no longer faced with the threat of sabre-toothed tigers, yet the same stress mechanism is triggered when we we are faced by our modern lifestyles or become overloaded. If this mechanism is triggered too quickly, or when there are too many stressors acting on us at any one time, adrenalin builds up and it can undermine a person's mental and physical health and actually begin to cause us harm, or we become ill.

So, let us now take a good look at one of the problems with all of this. We usually wear stress like a badge of honour.

How many times have we made statements such as "I thrive under stress!"? "I do better when I'm under stress!" "I am so stressed!" "I don't know what to do; my stress levels are so high!"? And the truth of the matter is that we are in those situations and those predicaments because we choose to be. It doesn't have to define who we are though. Or how we live.

Studies over millennia have shown how bad stress is for us. Over the last 20 to 25 years, we've noted in the medical industry, how stress levels are increasing year on year. We all talk about the world becoming a smaller place, which is true. It is becoming a smaller place. But, as the world shrinks, so much more is being expected from every one of us. We're on call 24 hours a day with cellular phones, email, WhatsApp, Facebook, short messages and many others. We're even available at all hours on platforms such as Skype and any other online form of communication and digital media

We don't have the same luxury our parents and grandparents had, which was a simple life with going to work, working from 9 to 5, and then going back hom and switching off, only having to worry about things again the next day.

So, what is it all about?

It's all about learning to cope — not changing things, not even necessarily fixing things, but simply learning the tricks and techniques that will ultimately help you learn how to cope.

Let me take myself as an example. Here I am, very late at night, still working on this book, after already having already put in a full day of work. Am I complaining? No, I'm not complaining. I'm merely pointing out that it doesn't ever end. It's ongoing, ongoing, ongoing, unless, of course, we choose break the cycle and draw that line in the sand.

I am self-employed and because of that, combined with the fact that I have a home office, and a family, I feel as though I never get to leave work behind. I choose to allow work time and playtime to become intertwined. But there's the key word – choice. I do this by choice. After having worked a hard week and most of the previous weekend as well, I have chosen to make this coming weekend a long weekend for myself. I'm turning my computer off when I'm done for the day on Thursday and will only be switching it back on and looking at it again on Monday morning. It's time to be selfish and focus on myself now — three days of doing what brings peace, harmony, and tranquility into my life is what is called for right now

In the previous relationship I was in, my partner and I began to realise, after a slightly crazy month, just how exhausted and drained we both were. In fact we were just done and at the edge of total burn-out. We knew it was not healthy, either for ourselves or for the relationship, to be in this space, and that we needed to do something about it. But what?

Well, we decided that the best idea would be to simply go away for a weekend. She asked her boss for few days leave, I asked mine (yes, I was my own boss, and that is often the worst task-master you could ever have) and the following week we went away.

Nothing fancy at all, just my bakkie (pick-up) loaded with camping gear, food and drink, and a short-ish 2-hour drive out of town to a seaside campsite was all it took. We arrived at the campsite, unpacked all our stuff, and then simply did nothing else from midday, Friday till late afternoon, Sunday. Monday, it was back at work, but one of the things we both came to realise was just how much better we both felt by the time we went back to work, leading to us both being much more able to cope with life's stressors and challenges..

Within that week, we resolved to make a weekend getaway a regular occurrence, and for the rest of our time together, we went away for a long weekend every six weeks. It was great and became one of the little highlights that we really came to look forward to.

So, what are you choosing to do to make yourself, your spouse and your family feel special?

If you would like some tips on how to get that mental break, how to actually embrace the stress in your lives, keep reading because, from the next chapter on, we are going to start looking at some different steps that you can take to take your stress levels from something negative that is imploding in your life to something you can work with and actually learn to embrace. After all, stress really doesn't have to break you down and leave you tired and irritable. You can rise above it.

As I've mentioned before, this book is set out in the form of a self-help manual, with each chapter presenting an idea that will help you look at and manage your stress Each chapter is based on the letters of the alphabet, and are designed for you to read, digest and then do the activity provided at the end. This is what I'd advise you to do if you want to go the extra mile, deal with stress and thereby get the full benefits from this book.

In the table below, I want you to fill in the top 8 fun activities that you would like to do or take part in, but that you feel life is stopping you from getting to do.

	Activity	By when
1		
2		
3		
4		
5		
6		
7		
8		

Chapter 2

Why is Stress always perceived as being something negative?

"Stress doesn't come from your boss, spouse, or circumstances. It comes from your thoughts about these circumstances." - A Bernstein

When we talk about stress, the first thing we tend to think about is something negative, do we not?

But let me assure you that it not always like that. Yes, we all know and have experienced that weird feeling called stress. But let me tell you that feeling stressed out can sometimes feel perfectly normal, especially if it's a state you've become used to being in and don't even really realise that you're in. You might notice that sometimes being stressed out motivates you to focus on your work, yet at other times, you feel incredibly overwhelmed and can't concentrate on anything at all. While stress affects everyone in different ways, there are two major types of

stress: stress that's beneficial and motivating —
or what we call, "good stress" — and stress that
causes anxiety and even health problems — or
better knows as "bad stress". Here's more on
the benefits and side effects of stress and how to
tell if you're experiencing too much stress at any
given time

After all, we all know that stress has been
referred to as the number one killer in the
world!

More people suffer from stress than anything
else and stress, according to medical research, is
also the one thing that is the gateway to other
illnesses such as heart disease, problems with
your liver and your kidneys, as well as muscle
aches and pains.

In other words, stress stresses your body.

But what if; just what if …

You see, for many years, the alternative
therapies, the therapies that are not main-stream
therapies have been saying certain things
around stress; certain things such as, "What
your mind perceives, your body conceives."

Studies nowadays, scientific studies, with
research that has been scientifically proven in

America have shown that there is a large truth to this.

In fact, not only do the studies show a large truth to it, but they also show an advantage – yes, an Advantage! – to having stress!

Now...

What could those advantages be, I hear you ask?

According to experts, stress is the source of energy that informs you where steps need to begin to start from. of the steps to be taken. In small doses, stress has many benefits. For example, stress can help you face your everyday challenges and motivate you to achieve your goals. Stress can help you perform your tasks more effectively. It can even increase memory.

Stress is also a vital warning system that triggers a fight or escape reflex, when we feel we're being threatened in any way. When the brain detects some stress, it begins to flood the body with chemicals such as epinephrine, norepinephrine and cortisol. This creates various reactions, such as an increase in blood pressure and heart rate. Also, the sensors suddenly focus, like a laser beam, which trigger you into being able to avoid situations of physical harm, such as causing you to jump or move out of the way of an oncoming car or ducking when a stray ball comes flying your way. In this way, the stress, though short-lived, actually helps you to safe and protected.

It is important to realise that, although these studies show that there is an advantage to having stress, many studies also show the disadvantages of stress as well. What does it all boil down to?

It all boils down to the attitude of mind.

It all boils down to the way we choose to perceive things because that is how our body conceives things.

So, what I'm going to be doing throughout the following chapters of this book, is start unpacking exactly what that is. I will, for those of you who are interested and follow, be giving more and more advice and results-driven information with stuff for you to implement so that you can embrace all of this. So that, when the new year or month or even week arrives, you're starting from an awesomely positive perspective rather than the, "Ho hum. Another year/month/week/day, still drowning in the same old nonsense" perspective.

As they say, there's no time like the present, so let's get going on creating positive change in your life.

List eight things that will be different in your life once you have achieved your goal of managing your stress with ease — taking note of when you think each of these changes would be likely to become a part of your reality?

	What is different?	Achieved Date
1		
2		
3		
4		
5		
6		
7		
8		

Chapter 3

A

"The first step toward change is awareness. The second is acceptance." - Nathan Brandon

The first letter we are going to be talking about or focusing on is the letter A. According to my expertise, I label it, ACCEPTANCE.

Sometimes we see ourselves as an observer of other people's lives, and we think that we will never experience what they're experiencing, whether it's a positive or negative situation. It is easy to fall into the trap of believing that this will never happen to you.

The real beauty of life is that it is unpredictable. Nothing is permanent. Everything changes; and of course, a lot of things can and will happen that will ultimately transform who you are and who you become. This is bound to have an impact on your life. The problem is that we need to cultivate the ability to accept whatever comes and embrace it truly.

You see, far too often, we spend so much of our time, effort and energy, fighting and struggling against stress and stress management that it builds up the stress within us; it exacerbates it because we get stressed about the fact that we have stress — all of a sudden finding ourselves on that eternal hamster wheel just going round and round.

I used to be involved in leadership training, helping to coach people through their problems. One particular person, whom we will call John, was very apprehensive about taking on the role of and all the associated responsibility that came with the role of being a great leader. He had shown great aptitude and ability to become a leader within the company he was working for. His bosses had seen it, yet, his lack of self-belief meant he was unable to see it himself and his sense of self-doubt belied his actual capabilities. The more he thought about his responsibilities, the higher his stress levels shot, and this was before he was even actually in the position.

It is so very easy for negative thoughts to grow within us and overwhelm us and John was feeling this big time. I worked with him over a number of weeks and managed, eventually, to help him understand and accept the fact that he is, in fact, a great and capable leader. All he had to do was believe it. We worked together on many levels with the common underlying subject always being about acceptance.

As soon as John was able to accept and embrace what his bosses had seen in him all along, and he had gained a clear understanding of his new role and all that it entailed, he was able to achieve his goals and feel safe and, as a result, his stress levels around these issues plummeted. Yes, with the new position he now had within the company he did face many challenges and sometimes highly stressful situations, having to make some interesting choices, but at least he found that, by accepting that stress was a normal feeling, within limits, and believing that he could rise above this, he found that he was able to take better control, instead of letting the stress take control of him. As he felt that he was taking control, his acceptance levels increased, and this helped him cope far easier with the emotions he was feeling within.

What about you?

What would happen if we could all get over our negative self belief and prejudices that we've built up against ourselves? What if we accepted not only ourselves, but also our stress ? Are you accepting of a situation? Because the minute you accept a situation, what you're doing is you are saying to yourself, it's not that bad, I'm not going to allow myself to get emotionally sucked down into what may be perceived as a negative environment, or negative, blaming self talk.

So, one of the first things about alleviating a lot of the stress is acceptance.

You see, the point is very simply that, when you accept something, you're not saying it's okay. You're not saying it's alright. What you are saying is, "This is what's going on," "This is what's happened; let me deal with it in a rational, rather than an emotional way."

So, the first thing I want you all to do is to change your mindset to one of acceptance.

We are all human beings, and our minds often work in weird and awesome ways. Instead of always believing what we think, we need to be aware of it. An awareness can so often help be the switch to changing the emotion we have had attached to that event.

Often the stressful things in our life are those things that we have very little or close to no control over; things that often manifest from outside of ourselves

When we practice acceptance, it prepares us to live in this ever-changing world, where you never know what's going to happen next. Acceptance is like protecting yourself with your shield.

To reiterate, acceptance is nothing like weakness, nor is it a synonym for conformity or mediocrity.

We need to learn how to identify when it's time to persist and when it's time to accept.

One thing that makes acceptance much easier is to list all the possible explanations for why you're experiencing something.

For example, I once met a person who asked me to help him with a phobia he had. He was so embarrassed that he was afraid of butterflies until... I explained to him that he has Lepidopterophobia. Knowing that his phobia had a name and he wasn't a "freak" was an important step in his acceptance of his problem. At the same time it helped him feel more normal and accepting of himself and his phobia allowed the issue to more easily be dealt with.

List 10 things that are causing stress in your life right now, that you feel you have no control over or no way of changing at this stage in your life.

1	
2	
3	
4	
5	
6	
7	
8	
9	
10	

Chapter 4

B

"If you don't stand for something, you will fall for anything." — *Gordon A. Eadie*

What defines what who are?

Many things are based on the core things that help us define who and what we are our beliefs.

"B" stands for exactly that BELIEFS

A belief is an idea that a person holds as being true.

One of the most beautiful things about humans, if you're reading this, yes you are one of them or let say one of us, the diversity between us. The saying "One man's meat is another's poison" seems to jump out at me as I think about this. How boring the world would be if we were all the same.

And this is no different from our primary topic. Because we are all so different, we need to realise that something that can cause one-person stress may very well be a pleasure to another.

Many years ago, I worked in Kwa-Zulu Natal. It has a much larger Hindu population than that which I was used to in the Western Cape, and so I was quite sheltered from understanding what many of the Hindu customs and ways of celebrating were.

I had made a Hindu friend though and was quite excited when Sheik invited me to celebrate Diwali with him and his family.

To be honest, I had no idea what to expect, but boy I was in for a shock as some of the customs were extreme in my eyes.

One of the things that Sheik did was dance and sing and pray until he seemed to be in a trance state and then (with NO alcohol or drugs), started piercing his body with something I can only call meat hooks.

No sign of pain or discomfort on his face at all. I was rather freaked out by this and the fact that he didn't even bleed more than a bloodspot took my stress levels to another realm. Here I am witnessing him going through all this to show his dedication to his beliefs, and all I could think was "Oh shit; he better not asks me if I'd like to try!!!!!"

My stress levels were way, way high. I feel they were higher than when I went skydiving for the first time!

The fact is that we all have our own beliefs and, in many religions,, this may even be seen as barbaric behaviour. But is it wrong? Or is it just different from what you're accustomed to?

Stress is the same. We have through our beliefs created certain belief patterns when it comes to what does and what does not create stress in our lives. We need not judge others who are feeling highly stressed about something that we would perceive as just a small speed bump in the journey of our lives. How often do we "feel stupid" for allowing something to stress us, and we think, "but it shouldn't be?"

As much as our beliefs can cause stress in our lives, so to will stress be increased in our lives in we have a negative belief around stress. This is true irrespective of if our belief is about what causes stress or allowing ourselves to be sucked down into the negativity of stress.

There's a beautiful saying that goes, "What your mind perceives, your body conceives" and I do believe that that is true. And if that is true, which is what I believe, then we realise that when we have certain thought patterns around stress and around things that cause stress in our lives, our bodies start to react appropriately and accordingly to our thoughts. So, what if, what if we changed our belief around stress? What if we changed our belief around the negative impact that stress has on our lives?

Surely, if we do that, our thought patterns change and positive thought patterns create a more positive interaction with our body.

What I want you to do is I want you to know is that one of the key important steps in stress management is to change your beliefs and your belief systems because, when you change your beliefs and your belief systems, we go onto the next "B", which is your "behaviour". Your behaviour will start to change and, as your behaviour starts to change, so too will you create a domino effect rippling through all aspects of your lives.

As we look at "B," I want you all to know a great benefit your belief system around stress. The more you believe that stress is bad for you, and stress is harmful, and stress is going to kill you, the truer that will be in your life. Change your beliefs, and your behaviour will follow.

List five beliefs that play into your stress-related beliefs. (what creates stress in your life; what stress does to you)

1	
2	
3	
4	
5	

Chapter 5

C

"Some people create their storms, then get upset when it rains." - Norman Cousins

Our next chapters feature the letter "C" which stands for both "control" and "consequences". Let's first look at consequences.

We are often bombarded with news about the consequences of stress and the impact that stress has on your body. Although all of those consequences are real and are true consequences. So many reports are going around at the moment, around the fact that we can change our attitude, and the attitude will change the consequences of what it does to our body.

Although we can say stress is a normal physical reaction, it can sometimes have negative effects on your health. Don't allow stress to take over your life: there are ways to face stress and prevent its harmful effects.

Our lives are filled with highs and lows that generate some level of stress. Everyone is affected differently by events in their lives; as a result, what causes stress in one person does not necessarily cause it in another. Stress may be the result of happy events (wedding, birth of a child, promotion, and so on) or challenging situations (conflict, work-related pressure, mourning the death of a loved on, failing health and so on).

So, why don't we look at the consequences as something that can be positive or we can make positive? Many people say, "I thrive under stress." "I'm able to work better under stress." And that is very true. Many of the people in the world do. In fact, most people in top executive positions say that stress is what drives them even further and harder than how far they've driven and been driven before.

The negative consequences of stress are "shoved" into the limelight all the time. We just need to realise that we do have the option of benefiting from certain aspects of stress in our lives.

So, stress can definitely push you to go that much further. So that is a positive consequence of stress, as well, on our system.

More and more studies are being done on what used to be referred to as "alternative therapy" in the mitigation of stress in our lives. One of the biggest and most useful of these therapies that deals with stress management is guided visualisation.

What do we mean by this?

The more we focus on something, the easier it is for "our-self'" to create it.

Let us put this into context. Here is an example.

Let's say someone is playing a game of snooker. What do you think will be the best outcome? To sink all the correct balls in a clever enough sequence so as to create the highest number of points, whilst, at the same time, making it as difficult as possible for your opponent to sink more of the balls in an even smarter sequence and thereby, beat you. What you need to do is focus on what you want to achieve, not on what you are trying to avoid.

This could, for example, means focusing on sinking the red ball in a particular pocket, rather than on hitting the black ball (the last ball that gets pocketed).

You see, our minds are clever. If you think to yourself, "I must miss the black ball" your minds will automatically begin to focus on the black ball and our body will make the most minuscule, subconscious shifts in order to derail our conscious plan and begin to implement the unconscious one thus messing the shot up.

We need to learn to understand the power of our own minds and put far greater effort into what we do want instead of focusing on what we don't want.

When we do this and choose to create better focus in our "lifes" (no this is not a typo; lifes represent our "selfs" which in turn represent the following: Self-respect; self-esteem; self-confidence; self-worth) we will automatically have more control over our desired outcomes by cutting other people's power and control over us.

But I want to focus on a little bit here, is on control. Control and stress. When we think about ourselves and our emotions, we have to realise that we need to be in constant control of our emotions.

The minute we let other things take over our emotions, what actually happens? We allow the other things, or other people, to control our emotions and we've got to take back control.

Some people will say something along the lines of, "So-and-so has really, really upset me!" "They are causing so much stress in my life!"

You know what? That is a lie. It is you who is choosing to be stressed by what that other person is doing. So, what do you need to do? You need to change your attitude around who controls your emotions. After all, it is you, and only you, as an individual who can chooses to be stressed by someone else's behaviour towards you. You can choose to be upset and bothered by it, or you could choose the complete opposite and not be upset, or bothered by someone else's behaviour towards us. So, we've got to take back control. You need to know that it is very important to take back control of your thoughts and emotions because, as human beings, emotions are where we work from 90% of the time. Who do you want to be your puppet master – the one up above you, pulling on your strings?

It should be yourself. Learn to take back control because, when you are in control, you can, and hopefully, will, make more powerful and empowered decisions.

What things do people say or do that rubs you up the wrong way? Think about the things other people tend to do or say that just irritate you? Who do you tend to give over control of your emotions to?

1	
2	
3	
4	
5	

Just by acknowledging these, you are now beginning to take back control. Well done!

Now create one short sentence that you can use as positive self-talk each time you're confronted with one of the issues.

| |
| |
| |

Chapter 6

D

"All disputation makes the mind deaf; and when people are deaf, I am dumb." - Joseph Joubert

Now we are moving on to the letter, "D", which stands for the word "Disputation".

Now, many of you might not even know what I mean by the term "disputation" so, to help you out, let me start off by defining the word for you. The word, disputation, comes from the word, "dispute", as in "disagreeing with". But, contrary to what you might think from looking at the root of the word, disputation is more about debating a situation, than disputing or disagreeing with it.

In essence, the word "disputation" means taking a particular issue or situation and looking at it, critically, first from the one side and then from other side, creating an internal awareness of both sides of the coin, so to speak and then hopefully being able to come up with something that gives you a good answer, or the solution you've been looking for, because this isn't about thoughts or emotions. It is about debating an issue within yourself, embracing your logical thought patterns, and determining your own answer

What we've got to understand is that everything, no matter what it is, will always have a minimum of two sides to it. But what we have got to do is that we need to become aware of the fact that there are two sides. For example, when we talk stress management, often what happens is that we get sucked in to the negative aspects of stress. But there is always a positive to every situation too. And what we need to do is to become aware of the positive because, once we become aware of the positive, we start that internal debate going and, as soon as we have got that internal debate going, we can then become more and more aware of the ridiculousness of allowing ourselves to be sucked all the way down into that deep, dark hole of despair which is often a sign of stress, when it is far better to rather focus on the positive spin and the positive aspect of that exact same issue.

Take things as thin as a piece of paper. It also has two sides. And it's our choice which side we choose to focus and turn our attention to.

If we have that choice of choosing which side we want to focus on, why should we ever focus on the negative part?

Surely, we should rather have the urge to focus on the positive side? Sadly, human nature almost always will have us focusing on the negative.

But does this actually help us? I truly believe NOT!

About six years ago my phone rang, and it was my mother. She sounded very angry, stressed and in a state of despair. She told me that she had just been involved in a motor vehicle accident, and was quick to tell me two things 1) she was ok and 2) it was the other idiot who had caused the whole thing.

She was stopped at a red traffic light waiting for it to turn green when a semi rig with a trailer attached to the back was turning the corner and took the corner a tad too sharply, leading to the rear half the trailer smashing into the front right corner of her car.

All she could do was rant and rave at me about how terrible a driver the truck driver was and how she doubted that he even had a license to drive such a big vehicle. Or maybe he was drunk, or high on drugs, or, or, or ... and on and on she went.

As she was ranting and raving at me about the whole incident, I could feel her stress levels getting higher as her anger levels rose higher and higher. What to do? When I interjected and tried to placate her with comments such as "But look on the bright side of things – you're ok" or "thank goodness no one got injured" all I got in response was, "Yes but what about my car?" and other, "me", "me" statements from her. She was plummeting deep into stress now.

Luckily, knowing her personality, I knew what direction to take this to help her out of the negative spiral that she was going into. I asked her "Mom, when last did you actually have an accident?" Almost as if a switch had been flicked, she moved from anger and frustration to pride, saying, "Yes. I'm actually a great driver! I don't have accidents". I followed up with a simple statement: "So isn't it great that after all the insurance premiums you've been paying, you can now justify it?"

Granted, economically this makes little sense, however from a stress management perspective it makes a world of sense. "What?" was her response followed by a giggle and "Only you would think of that, Jason." I had broken down the stress barrier.

After that, she got rid of the associated emotion and her logical mindset kicked in. Now she was able to see and acknowledge the "other side" of the situation.

Did this fix the car? No. Did this fix the situation? No. But, what it did do was get her to become more calm, to stress less and to find that she could actually cope with what was transpiring and to do so far more effectively and efficiently than she had originally. I took her from stress to disputation.

Disputation is all about becoming aware, debating both sides of the situation within yourself and then coming to a conclusion, namely that "I need to look at the positive side of it." "I need to be more accepting and aware of the positive side of it".

Go on, I dare you! Be brave enough to take any issue that you're dealing with, debate it, find the positive in it and embrace the positive, for as you do, guaranteed, your stress levels will go down.

You do not have to always even believe the positive. Sometimes it will seem so "out there", but that is perfectly okay. What you need to do is become aware of the other side of this coin. As we said right in the very beginning of this book, awareness is one of the first steps you need to take in winning the war on stress.

What recurring issue(s) are you facing in your life that is/are causing you high stress levels?

What is it about this issue that is causing the high stress levels?

What positive aspect can you find within this issue?

Chapter 7

E

*"Food is the most abused anxiety drug.
Exercise is the most under-utilised
antidepressant." – Anonymous*

Now let's move on to our next chapter and the
letter "E" which stands for "Energize".

It is a proven fact that energy releases many
different chemicals in the body. The average
person may not know what the different
chemicals all are, but we do not need to know
their names in order to realise that need to
acknowledge how many of those chemicals are
"feel good" chemicals.

Realise that, when we talk about chemicals in
the body, we are talking about those chemicals
which the body produces naturally, all by itself.
Therefore, they are natural and not man-made
so they are good for us.

Two chemicals that I want to look at most
importantly, right now, are endorphins and
adrenalin. You see, what happens is, when we
are under a lot of stress, we build up an
immense level of adrenalin in our body. We all

know about the "fight or flight" scenario that our bodies go into when we are under threat through the release of the excess adrenaline into our bloodstream. Yet, many of us have not realised that we can add to this.

Due to the fact that we are rearing to go, energised to the extreme with the abundance of adrenaline, we do not have to turn to only fight or flight. What if we had another option? One that suited a more conducive result?

Let's add trend to befriend to this list. Not all people want to get physical and this is another option of stepping outside the box to diffuse a situation and also burn off that adrenaline.

The trouble with all of this is that, if we don't have a way of burning off all that adrenalin off, it sits in our body, and, even though it will eventually start to dissipate, some of it still remains which, over time, builds up to cause illness and dis-ease in our body.

However, as it dissipates, there can be a residual beneficial effect of some of that energy still being left behind, surging through our body. It can be used for good and taken advantage of by being used to fuel the mind and the imagination and give us the get up and go we need to embark on a project or task. Or to look for creative solutions to our stressful situation

Another positive spinoff of all that adrenalin, is to burn it off doing exercise. I know of many people who, after an extremely stressful day, or when they feel stress and tension building up in their body, will hit the gym or go for a walk or a swim in order to burn all of that excess energy off and utilise it to the full. After the exercise, they tend to feel much better.

Now, I know there are many of us – and I have to include myself here – who go, "Exercise? Urrgh!" Look at my unique physique. You can see what my attitude is towards certain exercise" and "The gym is not for me".

Of course, there are many people do enjoy a good workout at the gym, either before or after a full day's work, and if that is your way to de-stress, than by all means, go for it!

However, we don't have to do formal exercise in order to get rid of stress. Maybe there is some other physical activity that we enjoy doing that can also be looked at as being exercise. I know somebody very, very well who, if you tell them to go to gym and do exercise, will give you the most disgustingly dirty look and go, "I hate exercise!" I hate gym!" Tell my son to go and run for a half an hour on a treadmill, he will give you the dirtiest look ever. However, he is extremely fit! Why? Because he loves rugby!

He might not be willing to run for thirty minutes on a treadmill, but he will run for an hour-and-a-half around a rugby field with a ball! Up and down, running here, running there, and when you say, "So, you do exercise!" He'll say, "No. I don't exercise. I was just having fun!"

We've got realise is, we can just exercise and we can have fun doing it! Which, by default, happens to be good exercise. Because, when we exercise, not only are we burning off all that adrenalin, but we are also starting to release endorphins into our body, endorphins that are the "feel good" hormones; endorphins that are that part that make us calm down, that makes us relaxed and that makes us able to see things with better and greater clarity.

Just take a look at our "E" in the ABC of Stress Management. E can stand for both, "Exercise" and "Energize".

Get out there and energize yourself.

Be energized! Go and do something to burn off that excess.

Go and do something to start releasing those endorphins, because it's those endorphins that are the natural, beautiful way of calming ourselves down; of just bringing yourself down, relaxing you, without you having to resort to any external stimulus such as alcohol or drugs.

When last did you choose to do any form of exercise?

| |
| |

What do you enjoy doing that, by default, is a form of exercise?

| |
| |

Commit right now!

What?

By
When?

What?

By
When?

What?

By
When?

Chapter 8

F

"Forgiveness does not change the past but it does enlarge the future." - Paul Lewis Boese

The next letter of the alphabet that we have to look at here, is the letter "F". "F" stands for "Forgiveness".

Forgiveness is a word that we hear being bandied about almost every day and we might even see it as an easy thing to do. However, to forgive wholeheartedly and unreservedly, is a much more difficult thing to do.

However, we have to learn to forgive those who have created things in the world that have caused us stress.

Now let's view it this way we have been talking about forgiveness but what do we mean by forgiveness?

Forgiveness is not necessarily going to someone and saying, "Please can you forgive me?" What it actually means is us saying, I forgive that other person.

We shouldn't have to ask for forgiveness because, if we are living our own truth and leading a fair and honest life, then there should be nothing that we've done that we need to apologise for. In other words, there should be nobody that we've really wronged enough to need to be forgiven.

It is forgiveness that we have got to give others. Just imagine, somebody does something to you, or says something about you and it really bugs you. It's almost like that proverbial saying of, 'A thorn in my side.'

What happens?

You focus on it, you moan about it, you allow it to become all-consuming and, just like a thorn that is in your side, will keep on niggling at you and irritating you until you deal with it and remove it. Because, if you don't deal with it, but just keep acknowledging and moaning that it's there, there's a high chance that it's going to start festering and then it's going to start to become infected.

Many years ago, I owned a deli in Cape Town. It was a fun business and not only did I make good money, I also met some amazing people, some of whom I still count as friends today. Sadly, due to certain personal issues I was put into a position where I had to make some huge changes in my life and one of those changes was the work situation.

I had to put my business up for sale and after a few weeks it came down to two different people who had both put in offers on my place.

I looked at them both as two individual people and decided that I wasn't going to play the "offer me more" game. So, I made a choice and sold it to one of them. I chose to sell it to the one that made the first offer. Boy did I make the wrong choice?

After reneging on the conditions of sale with the payments and on how to treat and work with the wonderful staff (I had tried to make sure not a single staff member lost their job), we ended up in court. She had only paid me a third of the money and kept avoiding me.

Do you want to know how this turned into a really stressful situation?

In the end I won the court case but, when it came time for her to pay, she declared herself bankrupt. I was told I could take the business back, but after 10 months, she had killed it and now owed the landlord 6 months' rent. My other option was to sue her for the money –

after all she still owned a house. By now between the money she owed me and my legal fees, I was finished.

That night I had a dream; I dreamt that I was in my car and had stopped at a red traffic light. As I was sitting there, this woman she drove past me. I recognised her immediately and gave chase. All of a sudden, we were on a mountain pass. One moment I was right behind her almost nudging her bumper and in another second, she was so far ahead of me that I couldn't see her. All the while the scenery flashed by in a blur.

Then, as I came screeching around a bend, I saw her car, on its roof, the windows smashed and she was dangling half out of the car, suspended by the seatbelt. I stopped and got out my car to help her, but, as I started to approach her car it burst into flames and ... I woke up, cold with sweat. I decided right there and then that it was my subconscious mind trying to tell me something.

I chose to just let things go and walk away from the whole lot. Forget the money. Forget the deli. Forget her. And move on with my life!

Yes, it was a financial stuff up of note for me, however at the same time the emotional relief afterwards was priceless..

But, what if, just what if, instead of moaning, groaning, complaining and carrying on about it, you did something different, and that was, you forgave that person and you let it go?

That's almost like taking a pair of tweezers and pulling that thorn out. Because, you see, when you choose to let it go, you're choosing to allow yourself to move forward and to move on.

And, the minute you allow yourself to change your attitude and you embrace that forgiveness, your stress levels that have been caused by that thing, are going to go down. It is imperative that we learn to forgive.

We don't even need to tell the person we are forgiving them. If, for some reason, you don't ever want to talk t them again, or you don't even know how to get hold of them, just forgive them in your own mind And forget about it.

It is an attitude of forgiveness that we need to embrace.

Why not choose to honour yourself, go ahead, forge ahead and forgive? Let go and I promise you, your stress levels will begin to go down, compared to those people that hold on and continue to harbour the resentment.

Who do you believe has caused so much grief/hurt/pain/upset in your life that you find it difficult to forgive?

How much of your time, effort and energy are you allowing that person/people to consume?

How much more productively could you be making use of that time?

How is holding onto this negative emotion helping/serving you?

Chapter 9

G

"You can't change what's going on around you until you start changing what's going on inside you." - Zig Ziglar

The alphabet letter I will be talking about next is the letter "G" and it stands for "Going Within".

Going within could mean becoming introspective. It may also mean finding peace within yourself.

In other words, it means looking within yourself and getting an understanding about you, about yourself, about the thought patterns that you, as an individual, have.

As we all know, a lot of stress is created merely by our perceptions of a certain something.

I recently had a client that came to see me as he was craving the desire to be in a relationship. The loneliness was getting to him (even though he had only been single for a few months). He told me that every relationship he went into seemed to go belly up as soon as it reached a point of seriousness. He also admitted that it was he who caused the demise of the relationship.

We went ahead and did several sessions where he was encouraged to take some quiet time to go and look deep within himself and, as he allowed himself to explore his deeper understandings of his thought patterns, he began to realise why he was sabotaging himself. We worked on this and he has just embarked on a whole new relationship

You may be asking yourself what this has got to do with your stress levels and this is a very good question! The answer actually is, not much. However, the reason I am sharing this with you is for you to understand the power of our own minds.

After all, it is important to know how we can take control of our thoughts because, once we master and control our thoughts, we can begin to learn to control our actions. After all, every actions has to start with a thought, does it not?

When you choose to go within, what you are actually doing is empowering yourself because you are learning to gain that essential internal awareness.

There's a saying on which many aspects of psychology are based. "The first step in recovery is acknowledgement". I am not referring to acknowledging the mere fact that you have stress in your life, although this is the first step. Rather what I want us to acknowledge here is the cause or triggers of this debilitating emotion..

In the very, very first chapter, I gave a basic definition of wha stress is. But there is another definitions of stress which I am going to give you now and that is when things don't go exactly the way that you want it to go, especially when it is something that you are passionate about.

Why is it that certain things bother you, yet others just do not seem to matter nearly as much when they go wrong?

In truth the answer is one word. PASSION!

The higher the level of passion you have for something, the more stress it will create in your life when it doesn't go according to plan. I know that many of you will reread that last line and think out loud "passion? for my job? That's not true."

You are right, the passion may be revolving around many other things that having a job, earning an income, is able to make attainable. Very few (less than 40% of people, in fact) are passionate about the job they do. What they are passionate about is what they do outside of work. The things that have been funded by work. Taking away your finances greatly reduces your abilities to embrace your hobbies.

When you can allow yourself to follow the letter "G", which is "Go within", then you can get a clearer understanding of what drives you, of your passion, and of course, a clearer understanding about why you feel the way that you feel. And we all know that one of the very first steps in achieving the goal of reducing your stress, is to understand what the stressor is.

So, try it. Go within and find what it is, understand it and embrace it.

Often when we refer to "going within" people think about meditation. Yes, that is a great way to go within. However it is not the only way.

Why not take a few minutes a few times per day to just be? Do not be afraid of sitting somewhere, quietly taking a meander through your own thoughts and listen to what comes up.

Do not judge it, do not question those thoughts; just let them flow. You may even surprise yourself at what comes up.

Follow these 15 easy steps to allowing yourself to go within.

1.   Find a quiet space (this may be in your own home or outside in nature or anywhere in between)

2.   Tell those around that you do not want to be disturbed.

3.   Turn your cell phone off.

4.   Get comfortable (some people prefer to sit and some to lie down)

5.   Make sure you are safe.

    Take a deep breath in to the count of 4, and hold it for the count of 4 . Then exhale slowly, to the count of 8, until the lungs are completely empty of air.

7.   Repeat step 6 and close your eyes as you exhale.

8.   Keeping your eyes closed from now until you are done with this exercise, move to step 9.

9.   Adjust your breathing back to your normal breathing pattern.

10.   Allow yourself to self-talk and ask yourself those pertinent bothersome questions.

11.   Have moments of complete silence where you're just listening to yourself.

12.   This can be done out loud or in silence. After all, self-talk done in silence doesn't stop you from hearing your own voice inside your head.

13.   When you feel as if it has been long enough or that you have the answers you need to hear (yes, not necessarily those that you want to hear) thank yourself for allowing yourself to connect with your inner wisdom.

14.   Tell yourself that you will take one more deep breath and then you will open your eyes and be back at full awareness, filled with positive energy and ready to face all that the day could bring.

15.   Repeat this exercise daily; the more often you do it the easier and more effective it becomes.

Chapter 10

H

"The strong individual is the one who asks for help when he needs it." – Rona Barrett

In this chapter we're looking at the letter, "H". What does "H" stand for? Well, "H" stands for "Help".

And, when I talk about help, I'm referring to two different aspects of help. The one aspect we're going to look at regarding help is the clear and most obvious one – the one that everyone should know about and that is not being afraid to go and ask for help.

It's a very sad indictment of the world and of human nature that so often we see asking for help as a sign of weakness. However, it is actually the opposite, in truth, because, you see, it takes a hell of a lot of courage, it takes a hell of a lot from a person to actually step up and say, "Help me, please?"

That's true courage. Courage is going to ask for help and knowing you will get it because, although everyone thinks that it may be a weakness, we need to realise just how much courage it actually takes for some people to ask for help.

The truth is, on one level, you are respected for opening up your heart and asking for help. Those that put you down for asking and call you weak, they are often hurting as much or even more than you are. They, however, have allowed their own insecurities, most especially insecurities around being judged, to stop them from getting this much needed help. Much of the "jibing" is envy and fear.

There is a lovely saying that goes, "A burden shared, is a burden halved" and when it comes to asking for help, and getting the help you need, that's exactly what that is. Sometimes it's nothing more than just being able to talk it through with somebody that you trust, in a non-judgmental and safe environment. It can make huge, huge differences.

Whenever I think of asking for help, I recall a certain client that I had way back when.

It was a man who is quite well known in the weightlifting world. Let's just say he was one of those men that make me look petite (and, if you've ever seen me, you will know how hard this is to do!).

Anyway, he insisted on seeing me at a time when he would be guaranteed not to bump into any other client and kept reminding me of the confidentiality agreement I had signed with him. At our second session, having built up a certain level of rapport and trust, he started to open up a bit more.

I then asked him a question that I knew was a deep and probing one. He never uttered a word, but just burst into tears. It was one of those "cries" that came from deep within and went on for a good few minutes. Once he had opened the floodgates, he just allowed it to be - this is what we sometimes need to do!

Sadly, once he had calmed down and regained his composure, he was more concerned about the fact that he'd cried and showed a weakness in front of me, than embracing what had just transpired and working with it

In subsequent sessions we dealt with the issues and he kept opening more and more as he realised the benefits, he was getting from all this. The one thing though ... at the end of every session he would say "if anyone finds out that I cried like a girl, I will break you in half!" It was so sad to see that level of fear and the false sense of vulnerability he showed.

"H" for help.

Now as for the other aspect of help that I just wanted to touch on is, getting help with whatever it is that's causing the stress. Do you know that the people who have the least stress in the working world are those that have mastered the art of delegation? I want to tell you all don't be afraid to ask for help. Do not be afraid to ask for that which can help you on all and any level. "Help please", a magical and powerful set of words.

Do not be afraid to delegate to others because, when you do that, you're actually reducing your workload, sometimes quite dramatically, and when you reduce your workload, you're automatically reducing the stress levels you're going to have, due to the fact that you can fit what you've got into your timeline without necessarily being concerned about the things that you may struggle with. Struggle may mean you aren't 100% capable of doing that task, or it could simply mean that you cannot fit it you're your schedule. Or maybe, just maybe, you don't enjoy doing it and therefore it feels like a burden to you. So you can relive yourself of its burden by delegating the job to someone else. Take that stuff that's on the periphery and let it go. Don't be afraid to delegate.

Just make sure that, if you do delegate, that what you are doing is delegating to somebody who knows the job and who you know is capable of doing the job and who will do it to the best of their ability. Because if not, this could cause an even higher amount of stress for you, either through substandard work or causing even tighter deadlines.

The word of the day is, "help". Don't be afraid to ask for it. Don't be afraid to delegate.

What important tasks must be completed that you do not enjoy doing?

Who could take that responsibility over? Are they competent at that task?

What will you do to still keep track with that person's progress?

Chapter 11

I

"Inhale peace. Let go of worries. Exhale stress. Notice the breath. Connect to all. Embrace calm." - Mary Davis

Today, we are addressing the letter, "I". It is another one of those letters that stands for two different strong words. The first word we're going to look at is the word, "Inhale". Inhale. It's all about deep breathing.

The way the human body has been designed, endorphins can and need to be released more often. The endorphins are those chemicals within our body that we spoke about in one of the previous chapters, that get released when adrenalin builds up. but remember, they are also a natural relaxant. And because they're a natural relaxant, what we want to do is we want to create more of them in our system, and the easiest way to create more of them in our system is through deep breathing.

I am now going to teach you the world's simplest breathing exercise – take three seconds to deeply inhale, hold your breath for two to three seconds, and then, do two to three seconds of exhaling, If you breathed like that for anywhere between twelve and a dozen times, your body has released all of these endorphins and, as I said, the endorphins are a natural relaxant and a great way of getting grounded and more focused.

If you're not 100% sure what endorphins are, everybody should know what adrenalin is, and endorphins are the exact opposite, relaxing you, instead of getting you ready for fight or flight. You can feel it in your body when the adrenaline begins to surge, in fact you can "see" it on your face. You will get a more aggressive facial expression, much like you'll get a more relaxed and happy feeling and friendly facial expression when the endorphins begin to surge, you may even begin to smile both internally and externally.

An inner smile is just a happiness feeling that we can allow ourselves to create within ourselves. It is just a feeling where we're happy with who we are, we're happy with what we are and those particular points where we are not happy with who or what we are, we put energy and effort into changing and recognising. Or at least recognising what things we've got no control over anyway and therefore can't change and not agonising over them.

Take it or leave it, an inner smile is an extremely powerful and amazing thing. There are so many people in the world who have that inner smile and you meet them and you just think, they're so nice, they're so friendly, they seem happy, even though they're not externalising it. It may not necessarily be a happy moment, or anything like that. And you think to yourself, this is a content person; this is a naturally happy person. Well, a naturally happy person is somebody who has learnt to have an inner smile. Luckily for all of us this is something that we can learn to create within ourselves. If we choose to!

As we face the rest of the day, and you might be stressing over a work issue, a personal issue or a family issue … Just take a deep breath! Inhale! And allow your inner smile to shine through.

What "happy place" can you choose to imagine you're in that will enhance that feeling of your own "inner smile"?

Describe that place here:

Take note of one or more memories that bring a smile to your face and trigger happy feelings within you when you think of or remember them.

Does this thought or image make you feel lighter or heavier in your chest?

Chapter 12

J

"There can be no justification for choosing any part of that which one knows to be evil."
- Ayn Rand

Now over to the next letter which is the letter "J". What does the letter "J" stand for?

The "J" stands for "Justification". Now let me ask you this question: how many of us justify the reasons why we are so stressed and why it is okay to be so stressed. Why it is okay to be going through all of the stuff that we're going through if we don't really need to be going through it? Surely, by justifying it, we are saying that it's okay?

We justify it because we have chosen to believe in something called, "society's norms". But, the truth of the matter is that we can create our own personal norms and we can also create an environment that is conducive to us doing better, that we can do well in. So, stop justifying things by saying, "Well everybody does that". "Everybody's like that." "Stress is normal". Or any other of society's norms that are all pure myth.

Let me ask when last did you go into a library or a bookstore and look for a booked called, "Normal People" or "Being Normal"? Is there any such thing as normal, anyway? In fact, you'd find it a struggle to find any title that speaks about a "normal" person. The truth is that the word "normal" has an extremely broad definition. When we use the word normal to refer to people, what we need to do is to take into consideration that this is what's "normal" for that particular society or segment of society. Not necessarily for everyone else.

Even then, why would we want to choose to be normal? Why be ordinary, when we can and should want to be extraordinary?

Yes, certain levels of stress are normal, but it's not whether the stress is normal or not normal that's important, it's the way that we interpret it within our minds, which then resonates through our body that makes the real difference.

But, let's just take another look at the word, "Justification" and let's break that down and just take a quick look at the word, 'Just'. Nike came up with a truly brilliant slogan, when they said, "Just do it". In fact, it is such a really and truly amazing slogan that I want you all to adopt it as your own and use it! I want everybody to realise that they, too, can just do it.

Just do it!

What is "It", you may ask? Well, allow me to explain.

"It" is any of the 26 steps that I have outlined for you here using the alphabet or the ABC's of Stress Management that will help you to embrace your stress in a better way so that you can work within yourself to make yourself the most powerful you that you could be. Just do it!

Don't try and justify your reasons for being or doing it. Just do it!

Justifying is a cop-out. It's a cop out by saying, "Yes, well, everyone is like that," "Yes well, this is normal." "Yes, well, it is not my fault but it is because of these circumstances." "yes, but it is ... (fill in a name here) fault"

Don't justify, just do it. Whether it is any of the steps that we've covered before or whether it is any of the ones that I'm going to be doing shortly, just get up off your backside and do what you know is best for you and for your body, not what everyone else does or says. Be uniquely you, because when you do take these steps, your desire to keep reducing your stress increases, as it feels so liberating. It is awesome, so don't procrastinate, do it.

"J," reminds us, just do it and Justification.

I was at a social gathering and as was expected, I met some new faces and was asked that most clichéd and boring question, (well besides asking about the weather) "So, what do you do?"

I replied with, "I help people manage stress so that they can live a better life on all levels" I got a quizzical look, which was then followed up with the usual comment: "But, we can't control stress. It is a normal fact of life and everyone suffers from it, to a greater or lesser extent, depending on how lucky we are."

Really?

Is it normal?

It doesn't have to be.

After all, life is full of choices; if we choose to be the person that steps outside of the mold, isn't it a good thing?

That is what a trailblazer is after all.

Ask yourself: Do you want to be a Justificator or a Trailblazer?

Which has a better ring to it? And which has the greatest chance of being both happier and healthier?

List three things that you know are helping you hold onto stress that you accept as normal.

1	
2	
3	

What decisions can you make today to change these negative beliefs?

Rewrite these negative beliefs into a statement that includes the opposite message. (ie, write it out as a more positive statement)

1	
2	
3	

Chapter 13

K

"Life is tough, my darling, but so are you. Keep going." - Stephanie Bennett Henry

The next alphabet letter that we will be discussing is the letter "K," and it stands for, "Keep going."

There's a famous quote by a wise man who we quote so often for giving famous quotes, and his name is Winston Churchill. He said, 'if you find yourself in Hell, just keep moving, until you've passed through it." And that why I keep emphasising the fact that stress management is very important and similar to Churchill's quote.

You see, we find ourselves in stressful situations regularly. And when we do we need to understand that this is just one of those little harder part of life, We're never going to live in a bubble, in a cocoon, where we are just going to wander through life in a state of total bliss, in complete denial of the truth of the world out there. We need to know that we will always be influenced by the outside world, and that life is never going to throw things at us, from without irrespective of how we feel within.

However, it is important too realise is that, at some stage, everything, everything changes. Everything comes right, and everything ends. It may not always feel as if it is "coming right," and that is often because we have not chosen to adapt to our new realities. When we do, we begin to create a level of peace within. As Ghandi once said, "This, too, shall pass."

I want to tell you that there is nothing that does not have an ending to it, and we can choose to either allow ourselves to get bogged down with where we are and with what we are stuck in, or we can choose to push on and just keep riding through until we come out on the other side.

It's your choice; it's my choice. Each and every one of us has that choice. And the moment we acknowledge that we have the choice, that is the moment we automatically give ourselves the power and the strength to carry on and to go that little bit further.

Keep going. Keep moving; just go through. Do not stop, because you will get out on the other side.

Do you know that it's actually a fallacy that quick-sand sucks you down, and sucks you under when you land in it? The truth of the matter is, quick-sand, in direct opposition to its actual name, is an exceptionally slow thing. What do I mean by a slow thing?

Well, allow me to explain. When you step or fall into quicksand, you don't just sink straight down. No. But you do get stuck and the worst mistake you can make is to struggle to get unstuck because you do begin to slowly sink and, as you wriggle and thrash around, struggling to get out, all it it speed up that sinking process.

People that don't get so stuck in the quicksand that they can't get out again are those that keep edging slowly towards the edge and not struggling to get out. They stay calm and focus on the actual goal of managing to get themselves to freedom, as opposed to allowing themselves to fight and give in to the panic that arises, so that they actually begin to lose focus.

Instead of just sitting there, wallowing in their own sorrow, and going, "Woe is me" and, "Well this is what must have been intended for me." rather take the more pro-active view and just keep moving. But slowly!

Do you know someone who has a mantra that goes something like, "Why does this always happen to me? I must be cursed!", or "I must have been such a terrible person in my previous life to be finding myself in this situation now," Maybe it is you who says that?

Why do you want to choose to stay in that emotional space? Allow yourself by permitting yourself to let this negative, self-destructive belief go and choose to move forward.

One of the biggest fears we have in life is called Xenophobia. We often mistakenly think it is the fear of foreigners. However it is defined as "Irrational fear of a person, group of people or an event or situation that is perceived as strange and outside of your comfort zone" Let me simplify it down to the fear of the unknown.

When we choose to stay where we are what we are actually doing is saying that I'm so afraid of the unknown I would rather stay here and suffer, because "better the devil that you know". Really??? What if just beyond that place where you are now is that proverbial pot of gold?

We must not fear the unknown, rather we should be turned on by it and thrilled by the idea of new challenges awaiting us on our horizon.

However, there's another aspect of the "keep moving" theme that I also want you to be aware of, and that is the physical-ness of the "keep moving" idea. Not only, the idea of "keep moving" as in working your way out of a difficult or stressful situation, but the actual physicality as in actual, physical exercise.

It has been proven, time and time again that, when we exercise, what we are doing is allowing our body to release those valuable feel good chemicals, or endorphins that we have spoken about before, into our system helping to relieve stress and just to generally feel good all over.

Did you know that physical exercise can have as much of a positive impact on your wellness as being intimate? Yes, I know for many sexual activity is still considered a physical exercise routine – and that's all good. No matter what type of exercise or fitness routine you do, just do it and stick to it and you will soon find yourself flooded with feel good endorphins and smiling inside and out.

Some of you might be saying, "Exercise? Oh, God??" But it doesn't have to be exercised as in going to a gym and exercising there. It could be something that you enjoy doing which, by default, happens to be exercised. You know, maybe you're a sports person who hates running but thinks it's wonderful playing a game of soccer. Or tennis. Go and do it.

I will never forget an incident that occurred a few years back with my older son. We spoke about health and staying physically fit. I suggested he goes to the gym and does some exercises. The look I got was a mixture of horror and could almost bore a hole right through me. His response - "No ways, Dad, that's so boring and sounds like hard work. I wouldn't be able to do five minutes on a treadmill, and I would die."

The interesting aspect of this is that it wasn't about the exercise rather about the fun, or lack of fun, factor. You see my son was fit; he had an "almost" six-pack without ever choosing to step into a gym. How may you ask? He loves sport; he played rugby, hockey, cricket, squash and tennis at school. For him running on a rugby field for eighty minutes wasn't considered exercise, rather it was just having a really fun time.

What fun activities would you like to attempt that could by default be exercise

What must you do to commit to following through with this?

What can you focus on today to help keep yourself from choosing to be stuck?

What one or two things will motivate you to push through when you feel stuck?

What can you do now to get this to start happening?

Chapter 14

L

"As soon as you have made a thought, laugh at it. " — Lao Tsu

Now on to the next chapter and in this chapter, we are looking at the letter, "L." What does "L" stand for? Well we all know this, but I will say it anyways, "L" stands for "Laughter".

I'm sure I don't need to tell you that, as adults, we simply don't laugh enough. And let me tell you, we've got to learn to laugh more. Laughter is an amazing, amazing tool that we should all use on a regular basis. Studies have shown that the older we get, on average, the less we laugh. The average adult laughs less in one week than a child does in a day. This does have something to say towards us becoming more jaded as we "mature". Maybe, just maybe, we need to learn to hold onto a level of childlike wonder when we view the world?

We have different types of laughter ranging from a smile to a "can't control my bladder, my stomach is sore", good and hearty belly-laugh. Now, sometimes it might be a real belly-laugh, and at other times it may just be a little giggle, but when we can choose to laugh at ourselves, at the situation around us, we will find our stress levels automatically begin to decline.

Have you ever wondered why funny movies, comedy shows, and comedians are so popular?

On a sub-conscious level, we are all aware that we need humour in our lives and therefore we are continually seeking it out. Have you noticed how many people giggle when they are nervous? It is a natural coping mechanism. In a previous chapter, I spoke about endorphins and smiling, giggling and laughing helps our bodies can also create these same endorphins and release them into our bloodstream. This then gets carried throughout our bodies, helping us feel good.

Laughter, therefore, is of utmost importance when it comes to helping us learn to effectively deal with and manage our stress.

But, when we talk about laughter, I'm not only talking about just laughing out loud or using the word "lol" in your chats. Sometimes it can be a little internal giggle.

As we have mentioned before in a previous chapter, everything in the world, everything, has more than one side to it. It doesn't matter how thin a piece of paper is, it still has two sides, and it is our choice, as individuals, to choose which side we're going to focus on.

Every incident that happens, whether stressful or not, can be looked at from two different sides, so why don't you choose to look for the funny side of it and have a giggle, or better still, a guffaw?

I am sure many of you reading this will think that that is far too flippant a statement to make when it comes to something as serious as stress. However it is not that you are denying the fact that the stress is real, happening or important, but rather, indicating that, if I choose to find an amusing aspect to my stress, I will find it a whole lot easier to cope with it.

A client of mine, who we'll call Nadine, contacted me to share a story about something rather silly that had recently happened to her.

She had been having a very busy day and was rushing, non-stop, from meeting to meeting. However, as it came closer to lunchtime, she said that she had begun to feel somewhat hungry, and so, with no time to take a real lunch break, she rushed to the nearest drive-through and ordered take out.. Not even having to time to park and eat, she had decided to eat her food in the car, as she drove.

As we all know, eating while driving is far from a good idea and even more so when you're eating something that is covered in loads of hot sauce!

Well, as you can imagine, the inevitable happened and, yes, that's right, some of that sauce dripped onto her top. When she noticed it, she grabbed the serviette out of the bag and tried, in vain, to clean it up. All that she succeeded in doing, however was spreading the lovely, orangey stain all over her blouse. Having no time to go home and change, Nadine went into a panic mode. What type of impression was she going to make, with hot sauce messed all down her front?

Luckily for her, she had a sweater with her, so, when she arrived at the next destination, on went the sweater, despite it being a rather warm day. Putting on her best smile, she walked into the meeting. . Her day, however, had begun to unfold like a "Wacky Wednesday" – when she walked into her meeting, they apologised and said that the air-conditioning unit was on the blink. After a while, feeling uncomfortable and perspiring profusely, Nadine felt she simply had to remove her sweater. So, while apologising for the stain on her blouse, Nadine removed her sweater, blushing all over as she felt the stares of both men and women present in the room focusing on her.

Upon removing her sweater, one of the other people present pointed it out and stated "Yay !, I'm so glad to see that I am not the only one who likes to wear my food," and promptly and purposefully dripped some of his coffee onto his shirt.

I share this with you for two reasons: one the other gentleman was showing extremely high levels of empathy as well as bringing humour into the equation. Nadine gave a nervous and, no doubt self-conscious, giggle and then felt her stress around the issue ease up a bit. Nothing more than humour and empathy had dealt with that issue in one fell swoop.

There's nothing better than having a private giggle at yourself now, is there?

Laughter? Embrace it! Go and have that good giggle and you will find that, when you do, those stress levels will start to come down and all of your angst and feelings of stress will be depleted.

Another phenomenon I'd like to point out to you in order to hammer home my belief around the importance of laughing and the stress-relieving benefits laughter can have on your life, is the rise of Laughter Yoga and the speed at which it has taken off on an international level. A rather intriguing aspect of Laughter Yoga is that you do not even need to have something funny to laugh at.

The way Laughter Yoga works is that the instructor teaches members in the class to begin by forcing a laugh and then follow a pattern - and yes, it does work! Soon the whole room is throbbing with the joyous laughter of participants, all getting a really good workout for their internal organs and, at the same time, getting rid of large amounts of stress!

So, go on! As soon as you finish reading this, go and Google something on YouTube that will make you laugh.

Think of a situation that increased your stress levels.

Think of another perspective you could take in which to view this situation.

Name six things that make you smile, giggle, or outright belly-laugh.

1	
2	
3	
4	
5	
6	

Chapter 15

M

"A creative man is motivated by the desire to achieve, not by the desire to beat others." - Ayn Rand

The next letter in our ABC of Stress Management is the letter "M" and what does the letter, "M" stand for? The letter "M" stands for "Motivated".

And what we've got to learn to do is to motivate ourselves more, learn to push ourselves to the limit or more.

Now you might say, "Push myself harder? But that's what's inducing all this stress in me!" So what do I mean by telling you to push yourself harder? I am not telling you to push yourself harder for more work, to do more or to be more under pressure of work than you currently are, but rather I am trying to help to motivate you, or rather to get you to motivate yourself to not procrastinate. I'm merely trying to motivate you to ultimately help yourself to get to where you want to get.

You see, the truth of the matter is that, as human beings, we will always work harder and push ourselves more once we understand what the reward will be for doing that work. After all, everything we do, we do for some sort of reward. There is not a single thing in this world that we do not do for a reward, whether it is a physical reward, a tangible reward, an emotional reward, a gift/donation and yes, even money can be seen as a reward.

For example – and yes, this is an extreme example, the reward for going to the toilet? You feel better.

Try to find the reward in everything you do, because, when you have a clear vision of what the reward is, you will find it far easier to motivate yourself, to push yourself to do the work you need to do in order to achieve the things that you want to achieve.

Back in my school days, all those years ago, we had Lady Chatterley's Lover, by D H Lawrence as a set-work book in English. Boy did I struggle to read that book, even though I am one of those people that enjoys reading. I celebrated when the movie of the book came out. My whole class went to see the movie instead of reading the book. Mmmm, say no more!

Remember in an earlier chapter when I shared how my wife and I used to go away for mini breaks every so often when we felt the stress was just getting too much? Well, it was on one of those long weekend breaks, slap bang in the middle of winter, that the following story took place.

Our initial plan had been to just go somewhere nearby to relax and be alone, with no kids, no friends, no agenda; no cell phones, no television, just eat, sleep and chill out. It was an amazing weekend, however, by the second day I had already reached the end of the book I'd taken along to read.

Luckily for me, though, the guesthouse we were staying in had a bookshelf filled with reading material that guests could borrow, so I had a look to see what books they had there and there it was, one of my childhood challenges, Lady Chatterley's Lover, by D H Lawrence! I picked it up and, over the rest of the long weekend, I read that book from cover to cover.

The question here is, "Why?"

Because, this time, it was a pleasure to read. Instead of a demand, or a "must", I read it out of a sheer desire to read it. Because I wanted to.

I was able to realise what the reward was, and this made it far easier to achieve.

This is but one example of being able to do something, push yourself that much harder, not to increase stress, rather increase the enjoyment of seeing purpose in the work that you do and to get closer to achieving the perceived reward.

What we need to do is we need to learn to motivate ourselves, because, as we motivate ourselves, focusing on and being aware of the rewards that we're going to get by achieving what we wish to achieve, we will stop procrastinating.

Human beings by default are lazy! Please don't disagree with this point, rather read my justification of this statement.

We will go to great lengths to find ways of making life easier for ourselves. Work hard now to benefit later. An example of this would be Josephine Cochran. She is the lady who invented the dishwasher. Why you may ask? Well, like most housekeepers, she wanted to find a manner of washing dishes that was fast, efficient and easy. She spent years working on her invention and design before she got it right. And the result? We have a piece of equipment in our homes today that makes our lives just that little bit easier.

It is amazing how laziness can motivate us to find an answer that actually didn't have a question! Ms Cochran was fully focused on the reward of getting the job done;, to her, the financial reward was merely a "byproduct" of her invention.

We will push ourselves that little bit harder. But, as we focus on that reward, we realise that it isn't that difficult.

Most of the time, we find things difficult because we are attempting or having to do something that we don't really want to do. You know, the mind is a funny thing. If you can be motivated to stick to it and you have a clear understanding of the goal you're aiming to achieve, of the reward you will receive, that motivation just flows so much easier. So, learn to be more motivated, because, the more motivated you are, the easier it becomes and the easier whatever it is becomes, the far, far less stressed you'll be.

Go on, I dare you – I double dare you – go and get a clear vision of the reward for accomplishing what you want to accomplish.

What would motivate you to achieve more?

Very few people are motivated by money. We are not "in love" with money; what motivates us is what that money can do for us.

What truly motivates you?

List five things that you want to get done but lack the motivation to do

1

2

3

4

5

What might the reward be for accomplishing these five things listed above?

1

2

3

4

5

Chapter 16

N

"Lower your cortisol level. The happiest people have the lowest level of cortisol, a stress hormone that raises blood pressure and weakens the immune system. Cut the stress – more yoga, less road rage – and you'll cut your cortisol production." - Dane Gilbert

In this next chapter, we move on to the next alphabet letter, and we are now looking at the letter, "N". And the letter "N" stands for, "Neuro-chemicals".

Now, when we talk about Neuro-chemicals, although there are hundreds of different chemicals in the body that we can talk about, looking at stress and stress management, there are only three specific chemicals that we need to look at and talk about.

And the first one I want to mention is one that everybody knows about, and which we have already talked a bit about and that is adrenalin.

What is adrenalin? Adrenalin is a special chemical that gives you a surge of energy and, as we all should know, it's what prepares us for what we call the, "fight or flight" response. It gives us that energy that we can then use as a booster for ourselves. That is the first chemical that we look at when we talk about neuro-chemicals when it comes to stress management.

The second chemical that we look at is called, nor-epinephrine. Nor-epinephrine is a very interesting chemical. It is a chemical that always comes together with adrenaline. In fact a lot of people think that it is a part of adrenalin. But what that does is it helps create a stronger level of alertness within us. It helps us to psych up our senses – our sense of sight, our sense of hearing – to work together with our physical body, which is what the adrenalin is all about and helps us create.

The third chemical which I would like to talk about, and the one that I find the most interesting when it comes to the chemicals related to stress management, is a chemical called Neuro-cortisol. You've probably heard of Cortisol being nicknamed the 'stress chemical' or the stress hormone.

What is cortisol? Cortisol is produced by the adrenal glands and it's a much slower release chemical than the other two. And it is all about getting us ready and getting us prepared and getting us focused.

What happens is that the other two chemicals are almost instantaneously there, in fact it is produced and pumped into our body within a matter of seconds, we're there, we're psyched up, we're ready for it. That "it" is what ever happens to be causing us stress at that point in time. Whereas cortisol, on the other hand, takes a lot longer to be released into our system and into our blood stream, because it comes from a multi-step process of releasing that involves all the other hormones within our system as well.

When we are faced with some sort of perceived threat, an area of our brain called the amygdala has to recognise that there is a threat and when it recognises that there is a threat, it then sends a message to another part of the brain called the hypothalamus which then releases this cortisol chemical into our system. This causes a chain reaction by alerting the pituitary gland that we need to release another hormone, and this is a hormone called the ACGH hormone into our adrenal gland, which then releases the cortisol.

That is the whole process and that is why it often takes so much longer to get into our system. Although it takes longer to get into our system, it is still an integral part of the chemical chain we need so as to deal with the stress in our lives.

What is this ACGH chemical and what does it do?

ACGH comes out when we go into what we call, 'survival mode'. It controls and therefore gives us the optimal amount of cortisol that we need into our system to help us to maintain the fluid balance within as well as helping to control and regulate our blood pressure as well as all of the other crucial aspects of our body.

When you have an issue that's causing you stress, for example a mental issue, and you are busy mulling it over and spinning it all around in your head in all different ways, what happens is, the cortisol is released. The problem is, when your cortisol is released and it goes too high, (when too much cortisol is released?) it is very bad for your body, and health because that can have an effect on triggering serious medical issues, such as stroke, heart attack and higher blood pressure and it always will, when it's too high, suppress our immune systems.

What we need to do is learn to control how our body releases all these chemicals into our bloodstream and when it is released how to deal with it in a positive manner to avoid the potential health risks.

How can we do this?

We need to learn to think without embracing emotions, we need to be able to shake it off, drop it, get rid of it and that brings all those chemicals back down into what should be called, our 'normal' levels. And, when they're back to our normal levels, that is when things will run far smoother.

The three neuro-chemicals all have both positive and negative elements to them.

We must also understand that there are two other chemicals that we have in our bodies – both males and females have them. One of them is oestrogen, whilst the other one is testosterone and those also play a role in how we react under stress. Far too many people assume that a man does not have any oestrogen in his body and a female has no testosterone, but this is so very wrong and far from the truth. In reality, both genders have got both, just to a differing degree.

In fact, it is the difference in amounts of oestrogen and testosterone that help determine the basics of the difference in chemicals of the genders. A person with a higher level of testosterone, for example, will tend to have a higher level of possibility of going down the physical violence route than if it is lower.

We've got all of these chemicals surging around inside our systems and all of these will and do play a role in how we respond to different stimuli. However, and this is what's very important, what we've got to do is, we have got to learn to control ourselves so that, when these neuro-chemicals are released, we don't let them become over-powering, overbearing and start reacting from a chemical imbalance that's now occurring within us, and that chemical imbalance is an imbalance to what our 'normal' is.

It is close to impossible to control the chemicals in our body, however what we do have control over is the triggers that release them.

This is important to acknowledge, as it means that we can choose, by default then, to control the chemicals by taking control of the triggers.

The best place to start is by understanding that we need to own our thoughts. As humans (I assume everyone reading this is a human) we think on two different levels. We think both rationally and emotionally. Rational thinking is often called "head thinking" and emotional thinking is often referred to as "heart thinking".

You need to know that the huge percentage of the stressors in our life (granted not all) originate from an emotional place within. This means that if we are able to move our thoughts (when appropriate) into head/rational thinking, we shall automatically reduce our stress levels through a clearer manner of thinking.

What was the most recent thought you had that might have caused your stress levels to increase?

Be honest with yourself. Was this coming from an emotional thought, or a rational thought?

In what way are you going to choose to reframe the thought into a rational one?

_____

_____

This will not "fix" the issue, but it will make it easier to understand and get a clearer perspective on what to do.

Realise that there may well be an appropriate time when you will need all these chemicals surging through your body. Try to recall one of them from your own history here.

_____

_____

_____

_____

Chapter 17

O

"It only ends once. Anything that happens before that is just progress." – Jacob Lost

In this chapter, we are addressing at the letter "O". What does "O" stand for?

The letter, 'O' stands for, "Optimism".

Let me tell you this: in life, what we have got to realise is that we should be able to see things from different angles and different perspectives and, when we are more optimistic and positive about things, things will run more smoothly. There's an amazing thing where they say that, "What we can perceive, we will achieve". Where our energies go, we will create a level of attraction, this is so true.

What I'm sharing with everybody in this chapter is, we've got to realise that we need to be far, far more optimistic in life, because, the more optimistic we are, the more we are allowing ourselves to be in the flow of positive energy and, the more we're in the flow of positive energy, the more positive energy we will attract into our lives and, the more positive energy we attract into our lives, the more positivity we attract into our lives as well.

The famous American motivational speaker, Zig Ziglar, once said, (well he did say it more than once, to be honest) "Your attitude will always determine your altitude!"

Is this not a real truism?

This does not mean that we ignore all the bad things, but what it does mean is we learn where to focus. We all do have the choice of focusing on either, choose wisely.

An example of that would be, take the people who feel overwhelmed at work and are saying that they cannot cope with the work and that they are struggling with their work. Well, maybe their problem is not their work but maybe their problem is their attitude both towards the work and themselves.

They are busy creating a negative belief around what their capabilities actually are. Or maybe it's not even their attitude, but rather their perception. And, if they can be more optimistic, they can find the positive aspects and the positive things within whatever is causing the stress in their lives.

My suggestion to everybody, is to learn to be more optimistic. Is the glass half full, or is the glass half empty? Well, here's the truth. It depends on how you choose to look at it. And, half full or half empty, it's still giving you something to drink! So, celebrate it! If you are extremely thirsty and you're given half a glass of water, you'd probably complain that it not enough. At the same time, if you were forced to drink something, you'd be quite content knowing it was only half a glass rather than a full one.

Learn to celebrate your life and celebrate every single achievement, rather than feeling overwhelmed and feeling as if everything is just piling, and piling, and piling up on top of you.

Be more optimistic, because, the more optimism you have in your life, the more positivity in your life, the clearer more things will run your way. An attitude of positivity will also help when you're interacting with others.

Many people do not read the acknowledgements, however if you are one of those that have read it, you would've seen that I thanks my ex-wives. Yes thats plural!

Relationships are interesting creatures with many layers and dynamics.

When I got married to my first wife it was suggested that we have a prenup, we both said it wasn't needed as we loved each other and it was forever, well...history says differently.

A few years after the divorce I met the woman who would become my second wife. Friends warned me about making the same mistake again, I did take cognisance of this and used my head more that time.

I have a belief that it doesn't matter what happens in your life, we always have options and choices. With every choice we make we need to understand that there are two sides, its our choice which side we plan to focus on.

I went ahead and did get married, we had many amazing years together, yes it ended way to soon, just like the first one.

However...

From each I got not only two of the most amazing sons, I also had many life changing positive things happen in my married life. Things I probably wouldn't have experienced if I had only looked at the negative and been too afraid to follow through with.

This is a prime example of how an optimistic mindset will have a positive impact on your interactions with others.

Recall a time when you were in a negative and pessimistic mindset. How did things turnout for you?

What could you have done differently to have made the whole experience end in a more favourable result?

Create a one line saying that will remind you to refocus on the positive. (For example: When nothing feels like its going right; go left - think differently)

Chapter 18

P

" I'm a pessimist because of intelligence, but an optimist because of will." - Antonio Gramsci

In our previous chapter we did already mention Optimism.

In this chapter, we are going to be looking at what most people would refer to as the opposite side of the coin, which is called, 'Pessimism'.

It is very important for us to understand the negative impact that being pessimistic has on our bodies, on ourselves, and just on our outlook towards everything in life in general. You see, what we've got to focus on, is not on not being a pessimist; we need to rather focus on finding that balance between these three states of being ie, which are optimistic, pessimistic and realistic.

Those of you who think, "Oh, a pessimist is just somebody who is always negative", well, that's not really true. The truth is, a person who is a pessimist, will always see the fault in everything; they will look at a potential scenario and only see what could go wrong. A pessimist is a type of person that starts almost every conversation, or thought even, with, "Yes, but …" "What if …" And is always wary of doing or starting anything.

All of the pessimists out there who are watching my videos, or reading this book, every time I've given a tip or suggestion about anything, you are most likely the type of people who will find a justification not to do what I have suggested; who will find a reason why it will fail. You will have given up before you have even started!

What we need to do as we work on stress management, is we need to be realistic. I'm not saying we must be an optimist who only sees the sunshine in every situation, nor am I saying we must be a pessimist, who only sees all the negative in every situation. What I am saying, however, is that we need to find that balance between the two and when we can do that, then we can say, I'm a realist.

I can understand. Risks are good.

A person who tries and fails is still one step ahead of the person who does nothing.

Now, when it comes to stress management, you might think, are risks really good? Well, here's the answer. A risk is good if it is what we call a calculated risk. What we need to do is we need to be less pessimistic, but we don't have to have our head in the clouds imagining everything going right all the time. We've just got to become more realistic.

When we take away all of that pessimism, all of that negativity, what we're doing is we are stopping ourselves from going down into that dark, deep place, unnecessarily.

What a lot of people don't realise is people who are pessimistic are so stuck in that negative role that they struggle to get out of it and see the positive, and, when things do go well, and are positive, they justify it by saying it's just a fluke. They justify it by saying, "Oh well, it just happened because I'm lucky."

The truth of the matter is that the more we focus on our negativity, the more we're going to believe that we're not entitled to positivity. And, the more we believe we're not entitled to positivity, even when positivity happens, instead of celebrating it and enjoying it, we rather wait for it to end so that we can be sucked back down into that negative state.

Stop being that type of person who, when something good happens, instead of celebrating it, and embracing it and enjoying it, you write it off as a coincidence, and all you're doing is waiting for it to flip over again. Rather enjoy it in the moment, celebrate it for now and allow yourself to just be awash with the joy and happiness of it.

"P" is a pessimist. The more pessimistic you are, the more you're choosing to allow yourself to stay down there in a negative spiral. So, go on. Start being, a lot more optimistic, with a touch of realism.

Write down the three most negative thoughts you find yourself having.

1

2

3

How can you turn these thoughts into a positive statement?

1

2

3

What can you do today to make yourself more aware of your pessimistic outlook? How can you change that?

Write down three ideas you can implement to help create a shift.

1	
2	
3	

Chapter 19

Q

"If you want the answer — ask the question." - Lorii Myers

Our next letter of the alphabet is the letter "Q" and it stands for "Question".

"Question". What do we mean by "Question"?

I feel this question is very simple: But we also need to learn how to question our motives, we need to learn to question our thoughts, we need to question our actions, we need to question what we do, and we need to question all of the processing that we have going on within us and for us when it comes to stress management.

What does this all mean? What does it all boil down too?

When questioning in general we can look at the following words: Where; when; what and, if we just change the "W" to a "T", we are guided to seek an answer. (There; then; that) this starts the mind shift to finding answers rather than being overwhelmed by questions.

When we look at our lives and we can question things – not question as in, am I doing the right thing? Am I doing the wrong thing? But, rather questioning it from the perspective of, " How am I benefitting from this?" "Can I let it go if it is not benefitting me?"

The time has come to look at reframing the questions we ask, so that we ask from a more positive aspect.

One of the key problems that we all have is we get so sucked down into doing things that actually do not bring value into our lives, or for us, or for our business, but rather because we're doing it for other people. And we've got to question our motivation around that.

I'm not saying you must stop doing all of these things. I'm not saying it's time to cut and not do anything for anybody else. What I am saying is that we need to question why. We need to question what and we need to question how it makes us feel, because everything that we do, we should be doing to benefit ourselves and the important people around us.

If we question things, we will stop doing certain things – don't stop doing – we will have a clearer understanding of the motivation for doing them. And, if we are doing things for the right reason and for the right purpose, and we are motivated because we understand that, our stress levels will go down. Why? Because we are able to gain a better understanding.

Too often, we go into an auto-pilot mode and we just plod along, putting one foot in front of the other, one word in front of the next, one chore in front of the next and on and on and then, when we come home, we're exhausted, we're tired, maybe we're stressed, we look at our "to-do" list and we go, "Really? A full day's work and I didn't get all of my stuff done? A full day, and the very key ones, that needed to be done, I just never got to. I need more hours in my day!"

I had a client recently who is highly successful in his career. Let's call him Bill. Unfortunately, Bill has an inferiority complex and therefore continually feels as if he has no real friends. (This actually is not true, but rather his perception). To him, the only way to get people to like him was to always be helpful. People knew this and so, when they needed something done, they continually turned to him.

After all, Bill never said no, because he knew that, if he did, they wouldn't like him anymore, and with the extra load of always being helpful and stopping his own work to do for others, things on his priority list just never got seen to and he began to get resentful.

This led to huge amounts of stress on his part, since, on the one hand he was so desperate for others' approval and yet, by helping everyone else out, his own workload was mounting up and yet he couldn't stop saying yes to people.

Stress was building, and the negative impact of such a high stress situation was starting to have a negative impact on his life and health, both physically and mentally. He came to me for help. It was a case of Bill needing to learn to say "NO".

The mere idea of this scared him, however I helped him to see that the side-effects of always being nice and saying yes to everyone else, and the stress of trying to be all things to all men, was even more scary.

He started slowly, (a journey of 1000 miles, also starts with just the first step after all), and to his amazement, people accepted his reply and didn't get angry or dump him as a friend. Some did, but then he had to ask himself, were they real friends then?

His journey to putting himself first started with one question, "Why am I afraid to say no?" When he found and dealt with the answer, it was the beginning of his journey to recovery.

But, if you question it, maybe it's not more hours in our day that we need, but to work those hours better. So, I want you to think about it. I want you to think about everything that you do and question it. This doesn't mean don't do it. Don't get me wrong on that. Question it and do those things that a) are important and b) will benefit you directly.

It doesn't mean that you do not ever do things that benefit other people as well, but it's just a matter of prioritising them. And you will not prioritise if you do not question.

Today, right now, I dare you to go ahead. Stop doing whatever you're doing and ask yourself just one question, and that question is, why am I motivated to do this? What should I be motivated to do that's going to bring a reward and a benefit to me that I'm not going to get to because I'm doing something else? And, when you have that understanding and you can prioritise better, and therefore you're able to do the things that are more important first, you will find that your stress levels will go down.

And the lower your stress levels, the happier and healthier you will be. The lower your stress levels, the more in control you'll feel and so you create a beautiful cycle that can go on and on.

Spend some time questioning what you're doing and, if the answer to the question is, go for it, then go for it.

What are you doing that's counterproductive that should be questioned?

Ask yourself those hard questions right here, right now.

What?

Why?

When?

Who?

Where?

How?

What are your answers, write them down below.

What?

Why?

When?

Who?

Chapter 20

R

"If you don't like to read, you haven't found the right book." - J.K. Rowling

We move on to the next letter of the ABC of Stress Management, we get to the letter "R". What does the R stand for?

Well, it stands for, "Read". What do we mean by "Read"? Too many people are under the impression that, once we have finished our formal education, whether it is school or studying a tertiary education, that once you're qualified, that is it. You're done.

But that couldn't be further from the truth!

Education and being educated is an on-going process that should never come to an end, Anthony J. D'Angelo said, "Develop a passion for learning. If you do, you will never cease to grow."

Yes, this is so true and the fact that we should be open for continually expanding ourselves with new and updated knowledge means the more we are able to further empower ourselves. If you have ever met someone who says they don't need to learn anything more, you have either met a liar or a person who is choosing to stunt their mental growth.

I have a friend, Bobby who is so passionate about books, he always states "What changes a house into a home are three things; pets, books and flowers! How true in my opinion.

There's a well-known saying that goes, "Knowledge is Power." How many of you have heard that saying? Plenty, I assume.

Sadly, that saying is a mis-quote. The true saying is not "knowledge is power," but "the implementation of knowledge is power." It doesn't only help to know what you know, but it's how you use that knowledge and what you do with that knowledge that makes the difference and has either a positive or a negative impact on your life.

What we've got to do is we've got to read so we're forever growing our knowledge base. So that we're forever evolving into more, because the more we evolve, the more we grow, the more empowered we are, the better we have the opportunity of becoming what we want to become.

And then, when we take that knowledge and we can implement it somewhere in our own lives, some way into our own situations and surroundings, that's when we have the power.

Now when it comes to stress management, the more the knowledge we have, automatically, the more options we have and the more knowledge and the more options we have, the better we can be. Not will be. Can be. Based, again, on whether or not we choose to use it. And the more options you have, the more opportunities you have of choosing the right one. So, do yourself a favour, never give up on reading!

Be out there and continually read and learn new things; let that be what is keeping you moving. There should not be a day that goes past that you do not choose to read something. A day should not go past that you do not choose to empower yourself. It's easy nowadays. You can have an app on your phone, which we all carry around with us all the time, with an electronic book – an e-book – downloaded on it. Instead of playing a game, whilst sitting in a queue, or waiting for your kids to come out of school or finish their sport, read a page or two. Go on, try it. I dare you! It's the most wonderful, wonderful thing.

A study was done with all the CEO's of the Fortune 500 companies in the USA. Without exception, every single one of them was a reader. In America the average CEO reads 48 books a year, the average middle management (one who has decided that they are at the level they are at is comfortable enough that they don't want to put any extra effort into, to take them to the next level) reads 12 books a year. The average worker only reads one!

We need to acknowledge at the same time that reading falls into two distinct categories. Some people read as a form of learning and other as a form of entertainment. Both are positive, which though do you believe is more beneficial?

When it comes to improving your knowledge base it is fair to say reading to learn is the empowering choice to make, at the same time though let us not diminish reading to entertain from our lives. A huge part of stress management is about learning to let your hair down and just have fun, to just learn to be in the moment.

If I invited you into my home, you would notice a huge variety of books. Books ranging from fiction (many genres) to non-fiction (many business books, psychology books and an area dedicated to recipe books. Add to this that if you looked on my bedside table, you'd notice that I am always reading two books at a time. One is a fiction and one is a non-fiction. Depending on my mood, the time of night, how tired I feel, will depend on what I choose to read that night. I have two personal rules: Never go to sleep without having done some reading daily and two, don't read a hardcover while in bed - do you realise how hard it hits your nose if you fall asleep while reading? Yes, it has happened to me (more than once if I must confess).

Has it not happened to you where you're reading and you think to yourself "why does this sound familiar?" Only to realise that you were so tired you'd not turned the page an had been rereading the same page! Hahaha (yes, another confession)

When we talk about stress management, talk about really reading, I just want to throw another little piece in there and the other little piece I want to put in there is, so often reading can also be an escape from your reality.

Let us just imagine you been at work. You're under high levels of stress and you take your lunch break, or your tea break, and instead of just having your cup of tea and allowing yourself to stew over those issues and those problems that you're having, instead of that, what you actually end up doing is you have your cup of tea, or your lunch break and you take your book and you go and you escape into the fantasy world of that story. What an amazingly awesome stress breaker that is! So go on! Go and read!

Reading doesn't even need to cost you a lot of money! Libraries are extremely cost-effective, with an exceptionally wide range of books.

How many books have you read in the past 12 months?

How many can you name? What/who are the titles/authors?

How many books do you commit to reading over the next 12 months?

Create a list of titles or authors you want to read. (including this one again)

Chapter 21

S

"I don't know the question, but sex is definitely the answer." – Woody Allen

Ladies and Gentlemen, "S" stands for that three-letter, naughty word that we all secretly love. Sex.

You might be asking yourself, what has sex got to do with stress management? Well, very simply put, what we've got to realise is, sex is not just about the physical act of sex, but sex is all about all of the peripheries around it, when it comes to stress management.

What do I mean by that? It has been proven that human beings crave contact, and one of the most precious key contacts that we can have happens to be intimate contact, i.e. sex. You see, when we have that intimate contact, and when we have that closeness with somebody, what we do is, we learn to release endorphins throughout our system and, as we release those endorphins, we're automatically going to relax.

Over and above that, when it comes to sex, we've got to realise that our body goes through all of these processes ... all of these changes, during that point in time of sexual climax and all of those things release all of these beautiful chemicals into our system, including cortisol which automatically is a natural, stress-relieving chemical. Why not go and have a look at what I wrote about the chemicals in the chapter on the letter "N"?

It's not really so much about sex as it is about physical touch and when we talk about physical touch, it often is more than touching in those erogenous zones. It could very easily be something as simple as holding hands.

Think about it. When last did you feel really negative, or full of stress, and somebody, irrespective of their gender, somebody who was a significant person in your life, just gave you a hug?

That's the kind of touch I also referring to when it comes to stress management.

This is no indication that sex is not also a part of stress management, it sure is!

What I am referring to is far more than the act of sex itself, though. It is not just about reaching an orgasm - even though an orgasm is an amazing stress reliever in its own right.

Think along the lines of a relaxing and long foreplay, something with lots of touching, where the only true intimacy is you allowing someone else into your inner space, for example, a massage. (Wait a minute what were you thinking?)

Remember, too that the sense of touch is not limited to our hands., We have the sense of touch all over our body. There is not much more relaxing and stress reducing that a long deep foot rub. No pressure, no expected outcomes, just being in the moment and choosing to physically let go.

Here's the deal. Go, today, and just give somebody a hug. And, when you give them a hug, just say to them, "You're special." Because that act, of the physical touch, that message of, "You're special", is enough to begin to release all of those hormones into your system, all of those chemicals into your system that will relax you, will calm you and help you with your stress levels.

If we talk directly about sex now, realise that the actual act of sex is the most wonderful stress reliever.

Try using sex, but just make sure that it's safe sex that you're going to have when you do have sex. Think about it. The power of touch.

I had a client who was in an extremely highly stressful career. She was always so wound up and continually tired and every muscle in her body recognised that it was tense.

When we spoke about the sense of touch and sex, her response was "I don't have time for that shit! The only benefit would be to make my husband happy". I implored her to give it a try. We discussed that it wasn't about penetrative sex, but more about touch and that there were ways it could definitely make her happy as well.

I suggested she tell her husband that she wanted 30 minutes of intimacy where he could touch her anywhere excluding all erogenous zones, and tell him that she will not be reciprocating (this must be before they start, or he may get extremely upset.)

She agreed, but I could sense the reservation.

At the next session a week later, she gave me feedback. Her husband agreed (I feel that he was also desperate for some touch, that would be the easy part of the homework) She felt uncomfortable when they began, initially, but, as the minutes ticked by, she began to relax into it.

She reported back to me that she has no idea how long it went on for as she fell asleep, but she was so happy and she had had the best night's sleep in she can't recall how long.

I had asked her to do this once as an exercise, however, I was told that they repeated this exercise 3 times in that week. I then gave her step two, reverse the roles and give your husband a treat. Far more willing this time, she agreed. The feedback at the following session was highly positive.

Months later they have admitted to me that they have two "sexual therapy" sessions a week. One is a time just for touching, with NO sex. They both feel it has helped them tremendously - the beauty of the power of touch!

What parts of your body do you enjoy having touched? (Non Sexual)

When last did you just give or receive a hug for comforting?

Remind yourself what it felt like.

How much more stress-less do you feel after sex?

Why?

Make a commitment now to embrace the power of touch/sex. And do it! Soon.

How frequently will this happen?

(touch, not always sex)

Chapter 22

T

"We have lost the art of sharing and caring."
- Hun Sen

What might the letter "T" represent when we talk about stress management? I said this because I actually know you might have thought of that.

The letter "T", stands for Talk. There's a beautiful saying that goes, "A burden shared is a burden halved." And that is so, so very true.

The amount of therapeutic value in sitting down with someone and having a good, heart-to-heart talk and a real, meaningful conversation with them really and truly does work wonders. It's been documented how beneficial it is. In fact, I can take it a step further and I can say that the foundation of psycho-analytic therapy is having a person talking through their problems. After all, is a psychologist not just a qualified practitioner of the "talking cure"?

But just to talk about things doesn't always work. You've got to talk about it in the right way. In the right manner. So, what do we mean by, "in the right way", and "in the right manner"?

We must all learn to just talk without being afraid or worried about being judged. And often with that, it'll boil down to choosing who you're going to talk with. You see, we don't always need to have somebody who is a good friend or close to us. In fact, often, we feel more comfortable if it is someone who is not associated with us. Someone who is not affiliated with us, because we seem to feel more comfortable in the anonymous value that it offers. The anonymity just works better in many instances. People feel they can open up to someone who doesn't know and therefore doesn't' judge them.

It doesn't mean you go up to a stranger and just start chatting to them. But maybe you need somebody who isn't in your inner circle, just to be able to help you and to get you there and hold you – not physically hold you, emotionally hold you. Physically holding you, we spoke about in the previous chapter.

You see, if you can be able to just talk and just be and, as you are just talking and you're just being, knowing that you have the comfort of not being judged, and you are able to just talk it through. And the people don't even need to comment or talk back to you. They just need to be there to listen to you. As the saying goes "God gave us two ears and one mouth, so that we would listen twice as much as we talk." It works. It helps. And you can allow your feelings, your emotions, your thoughts, to just flow.

One of the most amazing things that I've ever experienced was, I had a lady come and see me at my practice and she walked in and she started talking. And I kept quiet. And for an hour and fifteen minutes, all I said was, "Mmm", "Yes", "Aaah", "Shame", and maybe another few little words similar to that. Nothing more. I never asked her a single question. I never strung more than three words together. At the end of the session, she turned around to me and she said to me, "Jason, that was the most empowering conversation I've had. You are a brilliant conversationalist."

She thinks she was right but the truth is, she wasn't. The truth is, I was not a brilliant conversationalist. What I was, was a brilliant listener and I just allowed her to have the space to be able to listen and she was able to talk. No judgement, nothing. Just honouring her with that space.

Go, find somebody who you can be like that with. Find somebody who you can be and talk to like that and, I promise you, as you start opening, as you start sharing, your stress levels start going down. And if, just if, you happen to be somebody who hasn't got anybody like that, who cannot find anybody like that, feel as if the people in your life with judge you for showing a crack in your facade, here's two more choices.

One, you know how to contact me, you can find me on social media or on my website.. (my email is in the front of this book also.)

Two, instead of talking, journal. Journal is a form of communication. Writing is a form of communication. It's not as effective, but it is far, far better than just bottling it up and just storing it inside. When it comes to stress management, realise we need to learn to release.

Who do you know who is a great listener?
Someone who's non-judgmental? Create a list
here.

Write out a strategy that you will use to be able
to effectively approach this person to be the one
to help you.

What are the things causing you the highest amounts of stress? Approach these first.

Reflect on how comfortable you'll feel with this person, or should it be a stranger?

Chapter 23

U

"Understanding your inner self holds the meaning of your life." - Leo Tolstoy

The letter represents the word, "Understanding" and understanding is a key word, a key element, a key aspect when it comes to stress management.

Understanding is actually divided into two categories. So, let's look at both of them quickly. Understanding is all about understanding what stress is; what stress does to your body, what causes stress. Learning what the impact of stress is on your physical body and on your emotional state.

Understanding is empowering yourself through the knowledge of knowing what stress is all about. Of what knowing what causes things in your life to be what we define as stress.

You see, if we have a better understanding of the whys and the where-fore around stress and stress management, we are already on the road to taking back control. So, it is very, very important that we have a clearer understanding of what stress actually means for and to us. How do we define stress? When we can understand what stress really is, we will have a clearer indication of the direction that we need to take in order to be able to work with our stress rather than spending an over-abundance of emotional and physical energy trying fighting it.

That's the one aspect of understanding.

The other aspect of understanding that I would like to talk about is when you have stress, or when you know somebody who has stress and it is an understanding around that person's reactions to the stress, an understanding around that person's attitude and emotional situation, an understanding of why the person is reacting, or not reacting, in a particular type of manner.

When a person has a lot of stress, a lot of things change in their lives up here, between the ears. And I don't mean that in a bad way. When I say up here, we're referring mainly to attitude changes.

People become short tempered. People become so focused on something, that the rest of the world means nothing to them. They become quite self-centred. Or the exact opposite. They choose to disappear from the realities of their own world. If we have an understanding for them, a level of empathy what happens then?

We understand the situation they are in and we can show a different level of empathy, and a different level of sympathy.

On a sidebar, I'm assuming that a lot of people get confused between what the actual difference is between empathy and sympathy. So, if you do get confused between the two of them, realise they are not the same thing. Both of them can help a person. It's not that one is better than the other. They're just different.

To, show an understanding to somebody when they are in a stressful situation. Show an understanding to somebody when they are under a lot of stress and empower them by being there to support them, not adding another level of stress or a clash in their lives, and to be there for them. This is empathy.

To feel sorry for them and to offer words of encouragement but to not truly understand what they are actually going through, since you have not gone through it yourself, this is sympathy. The core difference, I believe, can be summed up as follows: sympathy is feeling sorry for another person, empathy is feeling with them.

In 2011, I had a client, let's call him Jeff, who at the first session told me that he felt like he was really weird. As I have mentioned before in this book, I remained non-judgemental and simply asked why he felt this way?

He started by saying that, even though he can think of no logical reason for someone believing that a pigeon isa dangerous bird, that he, himself, is more afraid of them than he is of spiders, snakes and scorpions all combined. He admitted to going into panic attacks if he has to travel anywhere and he sees a bird flying nearby.

I have, personally, never been afraid of birds, so how could I connect with Jeff and see things from his perspective? I chose to allow myself to recall how I felt when I am confronted with something that I am afraid of. After all, everyone is afraid of something… Just go and Google, "Arachibuttyrophobia". No, thats not my fear, but it is an interesting phobia to read about. This feeling I was now feeling helped me connect with Jeff on a deeper level, since I could now understand him and his phobia a little better and we were able to create positive change in his life.

When it comes to understanding, a huge step in Jeff's recovery was when I told him what he had was called Ornithophobia – the fear of birds. He thought I had made this up, however when he realised it was a real phobia and what he suffered from (yes, past tense) has a name, it made him understand that he was far from alone in this. It has a name, therefore there must be others suffering from the same thing!

When we can understand we are able to connect on so much deeper a level.

Look back at the Chapter on "R" and understand how reading will positively impact on the letter "U"

Create your definitions for:

Empathy

Sympathy

What can you begin to practice to improve your ability to empathise?

What do you fear?

Does it have a medical name? If so does this make you feel more positive and less embarrassed about being a sufferer of this?

Chapter 24

V

"When you complain, you make yourself a victim. Leave the situation, change the situation, or accept it. All else is madness." - *Eckhart Tolle*

"V" stands for two different things when it comes to stress management. The one thing that it stands for is the word, "Visualise". The second is the word "Victim".

Let's unpack these two meanings of the letter "V" in stress management. Let's start with the word, victim. You see, far, far too often, people play and fill the role of the victim. What do I mean by that?

Filling the role of the victim means that what you are doing is you are choosing to allow things to pull you down. It's all about you empowering yourself so you are no longer a victim. You see, when you go out there into the wide world and you're talking to everybody in the wide world, you're going to portray one of two things. You're either going to portray a sense of control and power or you're going to take a more passive role.

Far too often, with the passive role, you come across more as a victim – whether it is a victim by choice or a victim of circumstance – but you are allowing yourself to be a victim and, far, far too often, when you choose to allow yourself to go out into the world as a victim, it's actually a lie. It is you putting certain ideas, thoughts and beliefs into your head that are making you feel like you're being victimised instead of allowing these things to empower you. So, what must you start doing?

You must start taking control. You must start going out there into the world and saying I have the power. Whether it's the power to say, "No", the power to say, "Yes", or the power to do absolutely anything else in the world that you would like to do.

That's right. You must take control. Stop being that victim and empower yourself. And, as I said in]the introduction of this chapter, "V" also stands for "Visualisation".

What is that?

Visualisation is when you can see yourself where you want to be. I have already mentioned the famous American motivational speaker, Zig Ziglar and his popular saying, "Your attitude will determine your Altitude"

I want to reference that saying again here, as it is very true. Your attitude does and always will determine your altitude (how high you're willing to fly!)

When you can perceive yourself, and see yourself as the person you want to be, as the person that you deserve to be, then that's what's going to happen. You're going to start allowing yourself, on an unconscious level, to start elevating yourself to that level where you want to be.

You see, what the mind perceives, the body conceives. So, if your mind can perceive that, then your body will start to conceive that. And what does that mean? Does it automatically, like a magic wand, change everything around you? No, it changes your perception. It changes your attitude. It changes you.

You see, when you visualise properly, you do not change the view that you see from the room as you look out of the window, but you change what you choose to focus on as you look out of that same window.

Some people will look out of the window and see the weather and go, "Oh what beautiful weather! The sun is shining, there isn't a breath of wind, (I'm in Cape Town) There isn't a drop of rain! What a beautiful day!" And do you know what? If you're a tourist or you're on holiday in Cape Town now, that might be the most awesome, wonderful day for you?

But what if your business is suffering because of the drought? You're going to open that window, you're going to look out that same window, and you're going to be like, "Oh no! Another dry day! Another day where I'm not able to operate correctly and properly in my business."

Now I know those might seem funny, or ridiculous when it comes to stress management examples, but my point here is, how, when we look at the exact same view as we look out of that window over there, our mind perceives completely different things.

Do yourself a favour and this is the favour you must do yourself, start visualising things the way you want them to be. Start visualising the positive side of things, and as you're doing it, allow yourself to let go of that victim attitude. Let go of choosing to be a victim. Visualise your best life in vivid colour and with all the clarity you can muster, and your stress levels are bound to decline.

Think back to a time you played the role of a victim.

How did this benefit you?

What could you have done differently?

Allow yourself to fast forward 10 years, visualise and describe your new and improved life here.

What can you choose to hold onto to help to bring this into your reality?.

Chapter 25

W

"The day you stop worrying will be the first day of your new life; anxiety takes you in circles, trust in yourself and become free." -
Leon Brown

"W" stands for the word, "worry". Now, when it comes to stress management, worry is often a big problem. Why? Because what we do is, we're so worried about everything that we worry more and more and more, and that just exacerbates the stress and a vicious cycle ensues.

We often worry about stress and that exacerbates the stress levels. So, what we've got to do is we've got to realise that we need to control our worry, because, if we can control our worrying, then we do not need to worry as much and our stress levels will automatically be reduced.

A study was done in America and the study showed that, just under 80% - in fact 78.6% - of all things that cause stress with regards to worry, are things that we've actually got no control over. Things that, whether we worry about them, or we don't worry about them, they're going to happen anyway. And we spend all of that time worrying about something we've got no control over.

The study also showed that another 10% of the things that we worry about are things that have already happened, and the worry comes from running it over and over and over in our minds, maybe looking for another result or a "should have; could have; what if" scenario. And we end up worrying about things that have already happened.

A few years ago I had a client who used to get highly stressed when she drove her car outside of her neighbourhood. She knew how to drive and had been accident free for many years, however she got into a high level of anxiety when she was to "leave" her area.

She spent far too much time worrying about this problem she was facing and "fighting " with herself. She kept emotionally beating herself up over being "incompetent" at something "so silly". This constant worry did nothing to help her and her issue. The amazing thing was that as soon as she chose to not wallow in the negativity of the feelings around driving her stress less reduced and she found she became more relaxed and this lead to her finding it easier to overcome her problem.

Maybe there are things that we did have control over. Maybe there are things that we did not have control over. But, irrespective of whether we did or did not have control over them, they've already happened, and we sit and we worry about them. Why?

Another, almost 10% - in fact 8% - of the things that we worry about are things that we should worry about but we should have worried about them a year, two years, three years, five or ten years ago. And those are often things that are related to our health.

We end up getting stressed and we worry about things where we've already created that lifestyle for ourselves where we should have worried about them a decade before, so that we could have made the changes then. However, that brings me to an important point and that important point is best said through a wonderful Buddhist quote which goes like this, "The best time to plant a tree was 20 years ago. The second-best time, is today."

Those things that you're worrying about, that happened. You can't change what has happened, but you can change from here, moving forward.

Then the balance of this worry, from this study, are things that we do actually have control over. So, isn't it interesting that less than 5% of all of the stress that we have through worry, is actually something that we have control over?

Learn to control your worry, and realise that when we look at the big picture around worry, only 5% of it is actually valid and justified. Be aware of worrying about things you have no need to worry about and realise that, when you do worry, you're not helping yourself.

Rather look for answers and change it from, "This is worrying me"; "This is concerning me"; and change it in your mind set instead to, "This is a challenge! This is exciting! This is an opportunity!"
Think about that for a moment.

What worrying thoughts are you holding onto that are not contributing positively to your life?

What can you choose to let go of, even if it is worrying you, as you realise you have no control over it either way?

Are you going to let go of it now? If not now, then when?

I commit to letting go…

Chapter 26

X

"Our mental attitude is the X-Factor that determines our fate." - Dale Carnegie

The next alphabet letter we have to deal with here is the letter "X" and when it comes to stress management, what does the letter, "X" stand for?

It stands for the "X"-factor.

What do I mean by the "X"-factor?

Well, the "X"-factor is that little something that we all have inside us but often we do not acknowledge; we do not use.

Too often we think of ourselves as not good enough or we believe that everyone else is better than us. What we fail to realise that it's what we have inside ourselves that makes all the difference. And that little something inside of us is what we call the "X"-factor.

What do I mean when I talk about the "X"-factor in stress management?

There are a few aspects to just touch on quickly over here. The one is the way that you cope and you deal with it. Sometimes people deal with things and they think afterwards, I actually don't know how I did that, or I know how I did it but I didn't know I had it in me to do it. And what that actually is, is the "X"-factor kicking in, where we go into what I like to refer to as "auto-pilot".

In other words, we're not always consciously aware of what we are doing but we are doing something that is having a positive benefit and a positive impact. So, what we've got to realise is that we all have it inside us. But the "X"-factor is also the way that we choose to view things in life, and I'll use myself as an example. I don't consciously go out every morning, or most mornings, and say, "Jason, go and look for the positive in everything out there."

I don't do that. I just go out and see the positive by default. That is my default setting. And that is what I like to call the "X"-factor as well. Why? Because things happen. That's life.

One of the sayings I love is "Life is what happens when you're busy making other plans".

And, when it comes to the "X"-factor, it's all about rolling with the punches. That "X"-factor is being able to see the positive in things and to work your way around it. To be able to see what's transpiring and know that it doesn't mean it's the be all and end all of absolutely everything. But you've got to know that. You've got to realise that.

I often like to say to people when they ask me about remaining positive, "if you ever meet anyone who is always positive and life is always great, you need to question yourself, asking "what's wrong with that person?" Just as a person who is constantly negative and full of the woes of life, they are not facing a true reality either and probably have high levels (or should that be low levels) of depression. A positive person is not someone who doesn't ever see or experience stress and anxiety and negative things in their lives. Rather it is a person who has a higher than average level of EQ, (Emotional Intelligence) and who simply does not allow this "bad" stuff to pull them down. EQ is a huge chunk of the X- Factor!

Another saying that I absolutely love is, "The person with the most flexibility, always controls the system". And isn't that a truth, especially when it comes to stress management?

The question is, not "Do you have the "X"-factor?" but rather, "Do you embrace your "X"-factor?"

Mine is finding the positive in everything. This does not mean I do not see or experience negativity, rather I choose to not embrace it, rather to see, make a comment such as "wow that's an interesting point of view" and move on.

Maybe yours is just the extra level of flexibility. Maybe yours is being able to see what's lying underneath.

It doesn't matter what it is, just know you have it. I have it. Everyone has it. And it's a simple case of whether you choose to embrace it or choose to ignore it.

Here's a task for you to do today. I want you to go today and become a little bit introspective and become aware of one or two points about you, about yourself that is your "X"-factor and know that, whatever it is, that is what's going to help you and embrace it because it is all part of our stress management techniques.

Name one or two of your internal strengths that
help you cope?

What can you choose to do today to allow
yourself to see more of the positive in things so
as to allow your X - Factor to shine through?

Chapter 27

Y

"Your life is a result of the choices you make… if you don't like your life it is time to start making better choices." - Catherine Pulsifer

What does the letter "Y" stand for when we're talking about stress management?

Well, to be perfectly honest, I cheated a little bit with the letter "Y" and the word is "Why".

"Why?"

Why do we need stress management?

Why?

And there's a very simple answer to that – because we have stress! So the question becomes, why do we choose to have stress?

One of the key things that we need to look at: the word "choose".

Have you noticed how often I use the word "choose" in this book?
That's correct, quite often. We almost always

have a choice, sadly we also have a default pattern that we far too often get stuck in.

Things happen in our lives – that's part of life. After all, as I've said before, "Life is what happens when you're busy making other plans" We have got to realise is that stress is not caused by what happens in our lives. It's not even caused by what happens around us. Stress is caused by the attitude that we choose to take to what we have around us, how we choose to interpret what is happening to us and around us.

Nothing causes stress in our lives, except for one thing and that is our interpretation of what is happening around us. So, whenever we are feeling stressed, one of the key things that we must do, is ask ourselves, why?

Why am I allowing this particular incident, that particular person, this event to cause stress in my life? It's the most amazing, empowering question to ask. Why? Why am I choosing? And, when you can ask yourself that question, and answer it truthfully to yourself, it's at that moment in time that you will begin to realise that it is you that has all the power. And the fact is that it is your choice and all you have to do is change the choice.

We all accept that we have a choice when it comes to physical and materialistic things. For example, you walk into a convenience store because you are thirsty. You go to the cool drink section where you are faced with a myriad of choices over what drink you're going to buy. Do you get, still water, sparkling water, flavoured water, still fruit juice, sparkling fruit juice, with sugar, sugar-free, fizzy drinks, energy drinks, milky drinks ...our choices are endless. Why should it be any different when it comes to our emotions? Should the choice of which emotion to choose also not be endless?

No one can make you make you angry or happy, they can say or do things and you have the choice of how you want to feel in response. If you are serious about stopping stress from ruling your life, you will make the choice to take back your control and power over your life

I want you to realise that from now on, you must ask yourself. Don't just take things on face value. Don't just take things for granted. Question everything. And if, logically, it still makes sense to have stress, go for it! I don't know why you'd want to, but go for it. What you've got to do is not be afraid to question.

The letter of today, "Y", is the word, "why". Go forth and ask!

I dare you!

No, no, no. I don't dare you; I double, triple dare you!

Ask why!

Why am I choosing to allow it to have this kind of negative impact on my life?

Try it.

It's scary how empowering it can be.

What is the one thing you can start doing NOW to take back control of your emotions?

List five new choices you are going to start changing from today.

List 6 "WHY" questions you will begin asking yourself.

In a week, list three events where you felt more empowered and more in control after creating change in your life.

Chapter 28

Z

"You spend one-third of your life in bed, and a good night's sleep has such an incredible impact on how you feel." - Nancy Shark

"Z", ladies and gentlemen, stands for "sleep". Yes, I know you are probably wondering, how can the letter, "Z" stand for "sleep".

Zzzzzzzzzzzzzz

No, Please don't go to sleep now! Rather read this first!

Why is sleep so important when it comes to stress management?

The truth of the matter is, far, far too many people do not get enough sleep. When we were living thousands and thousands of years ago, we didn't have electricity that our nights and after dark, could be as productive as our days could be. Yet, we're at that point in our lives now where, both at night as well as during the day, we can do all the same things. We can light up our lives. We can cook late at night, we can go shopping late at night. How many places are even open 24 hours a day?

What has happened? Yes, it has made things a lot more convenient, but at the same time, since there is no more true darkness, our internal body clocks have gone into a complete tizz. What does this mean? This means that most human beings stay awake for longer and, even when they do get to sleep, they're getting far too little sleep or sleep that is not of a good quality.

But, this is not all about sleep. This is about stress management. But, here's the problem. When we do not get enough sleep, we find our coping skills deteriorate amongst many, many people with many, many things. So, what you need to realise is that a very, very important aspect of our stress management is making sure we get enough sleep.

What is enough sleep?

Enough sleep should be a minimum of 8 hours a night. Let's be honest, when we do get that amount of sleep, we actually are able to cope better. Unfortunately, how many of you reading this – and I include myself in this – do not even get close to that?

We sometimes "brag" to our friends, "Man, I'm so stressed and I had to work so hard, I had to push myself and I had all of these deadlines that last night, I only managed to get 2 hours of sleep!" or "Do you know, I had to pull an all-nighter, the other day?", and this is definitely not beneficial when it comes to our stress management. So what do we need to do?

We need to learn to sleep properly and for long enough to rest completely. And part of that means, scheduling a time to go to bed and sticking to it. And yes, it might be difficult in the beginning, and you will not sleep well, or you might wake up in the morning and you'll feel that you've overslept. The truth of the matter is, we train our bodies. So, start today. Make tonight that first night that you're going to go to bed at a decent hour.

In the 1980's and 90's I worked in the hospitality industry. In those days we often worked something called split shift. This meant that we started work at 7am and worked till 2pm (breakfast and lunch) then we were off for four hours and had to report back to work at 6pm after which we worked till 11pm.

I'd get back home around midnight and then was able to relax a while before going to bed and getting about five hours of sleep before it was time to get up and start all over again. After a while your body adjusts and you begin coping with the five hours a night.

On a day off, you'd sleep seven hours straight (if your kids didn't' wake you) and feel like you had gotten a sleep in. It has been scientifically proven that this has an extremely negative health impact on our bodies. Stress being one of the key issues.

And you will find, those two or three hours that you lost out on, you will easily and effortlessly be able to make back up. Why? Because you are going to start sleeping properly. You're going to start finding that you're therefore more able, easily and effortlessly, to cope with all of the stuff that's happening around you.

When you have slept enough hours at night, you will find that your productivity increases and with that so do your coping skills.

You need to make sleep a priority. Where does this start?

Have a good look at your bedroom. Is it set up to promote a good night's sleep? The three key things that stop you from sleeping well is:

Physical discomfort, mental discomfort and distractions.

Physical discomfort: this could be anything from sleeping on a bed with the "wrong" mattress, to being too hot or too cold in the night. It could also be a physical pain that is stopping you from getting comfortable.

Mental Discomfort: This is one of the most common, and is the one directly related to stress management. Mental discomfort occurs when you can't get your mind to slow down or let itself "switch off" and go into a relaxed state. How often have you gone to bed and thought about your day and started to doubt some of your actions, thoughts and decisions? Maybe you have a TV in the bedroom? You should be avoiding the type of stimulation a TV creates for about half an hour before you go to sleep. In addition, it is not a good idea to keep your mobile phone too close to your head at night, even if it is switched off.

In my home all phones are not only put on silent when we go to bed, they are also left in the kitchen (the only place we have phone chargers. Yes, my doing).

Distractions: this is a restless bed partner or noises from outside, neighbours or just the next door room.

We can easily see from children that we, as humans, always find it easier to cope if we have a fixed routine in our lives to follow. So, if you don't already have one, why not choose right now to create your own routine for yourself?

Have an awesome, awesome day and remember, sleep tight!

How much sleep do you get on an average night?

How much more would you like to get?

What would be a realistic time to go to sleep to get closer to your eight hours?

What new bedtime routine are you going to create, write it down now.

Conclusion

As has been mentioned several times throughout this book, we are not able to eradicate stress from our lives entirely.

What we can do, and actually need to do, is to utilise the correct tools that we have in our toolbox of life in order to help us manage and cope with the stress we do have.

The world is moving faster and faster and each and every person who has a copy of this book now has the distinct advantage of having over 26 different, easy to implement tools to help them to take back control rather than allowing life to control them.

My wish is for each person who reads this book to find those tips and tricks that work best for them and then to apply them, thereby allowing themselves to become the best version of who they truly are.

I am looking forward to receiving feedback on your successes in your stress management.

Feel free to email me:
jason@jasonsandlerspeaks.com

For even more information, please come and find me at www.jasonsandlerspeaks.com or on my YouTube Channel.

**UPWARDS & ONWARDS TO BECOMING
THE BEST YOU THAT YOU CAN BE!**

May the pages of this book become littered with
your notes and thinking as you begin to pack
your stressors and start to unlock your full
potential.